Rural Entrepreneurism

Rural Entrepreneurism

Edited By

Dr. S. Maria John
Dr. R. Jeyabalan
Dr. S. Krisnamurthy

DISCOVERY PUBLISHING HOUSE
NEW DELHI

First Published–2004

Reprinted-2011

ISBN: 81-7141-819-8

Published by:

DISCOVERY PUBLISHING HOUSE

4831/24, Prahlad Street, Ansari Road, Darya Ganj
New Delhi–110 002 (India)
Phone: 23279245, • *Fax: 91-11-23253475*
e-mail: dphtemp@indiatimes.com

Printed at Mehra Offset Press, Delhi

Preface

The Post Graduate Department of Commerce, Cardamom Planters Association College, Bodinayakanur 625 513 (TN) organised a two-day National Level Seminar titled *"Entrepreneurism in Rural Economy"*. In the seminar, many eminent personalities, Professors of various universities and college and research scholars have presented their research articles and papers on matters relating with the promotion of new enterprises, new dimensions, role of Information Technology, role of Small Scale Industries on the growth of entrepreneurship of Government assistance to entrepreneurs. Sincere and modest efforts had been taken in the present book by the co-editors viz. Dr. R. Jeyabalan and Dr. S. Krishnamurthy, Readers in Commerce Cardamom Planters' Association College Bodinayakanur to select quality oriented research articles and the same are presented under the title *"Rural Entrepreneurism"*.

The research articles presented in this book provide maximum possible information useful regarding the subject matter taken up for discussion. This book also sets out to provide its readers the global aspects of entrepreneurs. The perspectives of co-operative entrepreneurism also take a vital part.

We are happy to express our sincere thanks to the honourable management of CPA College, Bodi, the contributors, the participants on the seminar and all our colleagues who supported it on brining this task to a great success. Our earnest thanks are also due to Mr. Tilak Wasan, the Proprietor, DPH Publishers and Booksellers, New Delhi for the sincere efforts taken in publishing this book.

Dr. S. Maria John
Dr. R. Jeyabalan
Dr. S. Krisnamurthy

Contents

1

Small Scale Industries Facilitate the Promotion of New Entrepreneurs: A Ground Reality

*Dr. S. Joseph Xavier**
*Mr. S. Elango***

Industrialisation of an economy, hastens the process of development of the country. It adds, to the gross domestic product directly and also helps the other sectors to grow. It adds, value to farm products, through processing, grading, packaging, storage and transport, provides market, for farm products, supplies inputs to farm production and enables transfer of surplus labour out of agriculture and reduces man land ratio. Large scale industries are capital intensive and they create islands of prosperity in capital scarce developing economies. Small scale industries are labour intensive, particularly suited for better utilisation of local resources. Small-scale industries use indigenous technology and skill to produce, high value products, many of items are exported. Therefore, development of small scale industries, have received priority in the five-year plan of India. Small scale industries play an important role in the socio-economic development of the nations. They are helpful, in reducing the disparities, between states and regions, through their wide dispersal in rural areas.

* Dr. S. Joseph Xavier, (Reader in Commerce, St. Joseph's College, Trichy).
** Mr. S. Elango, M.Com., M. Phil., PGDCSA, (Faculty of commerce, St. Joseph's College, Trichy)

Success of Small Scale Industries

According to the economic survey 1997-98, there were 30.14 lakhs small scale Industrial units in India and they created wealth to the tune of Rs. 4,65,171 crores, they exported goods worth Rs. 43,946 crores and employed 167.20 lakhs persons. Over the decades 1988-98 the value of production has increased more than four-fold from Rs. 4372 crores to Rs 4,65,171 crores. Export increased almost ten fold from Rs 4,372 crore to Rs 43,946 crores, employment has gone up from 107 lakhs to 1,167 lakhs. Further success and prosperity of small scale industries depends upon efficiency of the entrepreneurs. N.S. Toor found the causes of stickness in the history of closed units. Of the units failed 35% financial, 14.3% marketing problems, 5.6% raw materials scarcity, 3.7% disputes among owners, 3.3% natural calamities, 2.3% labour problems, 16.6% for more than one reasons, 19.3% for other reasons like poor entrepreneurship.

Entrepreneur and Entrepreneurship

Entrepreneurship has a direct bearing on the growth, and development of small scale industries which will ultimately result in economic development. In practice, entrepreneurs have historically altered the direction of national economies, Industries and markets, they have invented new products, and develop the organisations, and means of production to bring them to market. Entrepreneurship is one of the four mainstream economic factors land, labour, capital and entrepreneurship. David H. Hold observes, "Entrepreneur seeks to reform or revolutionise the pattern of production by exploiting an invention or more generally an untried technological possibility for providing a new commodity or producing an old one in new way by opening up new source of supply of materials or a new outlet for problems: it essentially consists in doing things that are not generally done in the ordinary course of business.

Suitability of Ground Reality of India for the Promotion of Small Scale Industries and Entrepreneurism

The socio-economic and cultural status of the population

of India make easy promotion of small scale industries. Largely, the economic status of the Indian population is not high, literacy rate also is not too high; the prevailing and existing level of economic and social status is very much sufficient to become entrepreneurs of small scale industries. The rate of literacy now 1997 stands at 62% from 52.21% in 1991 census. The nature of literacy level in the country has no doubt increased over the decades, which provide a very good opening of the development of small scale industries. Small scale industries sector helps the promotion of entrepreneurism even among the illiterates, because there are certain industries having the cultural sound, requiring, only self-confidence, (e.g.) food product industries require general efficiency more than the educational qualification. The other supporting ground reality factors are risk bearing ability, management ability, family background, technical knowledge, financial stability, personality and personal skills, availability of supporting facilites and borrwing power of the people in general.

Strategies for the Healthy Promotion of Entrepreneurism in India

1. Generally, we used to say that entrepreneurs are born and not made. It is the high time to take efforts vigorously for the change of the statement, and make it as entrepreneurs are born as well as made, promotion of entrepreneurism should be the reach of every common man. Which facilitates self employment. In order to benefit every common man, a study of entrepreneurism should be included in the curriculum right from the school-level.

2. Problem of Managerial incompetancy is a serious problem for the failure of small scale industris. It is the government and other organisatins to take strategical methods categorically at the higher educational level. The Establishment of Entrepreneurial cell in all the College, Universities, study centre, district libraries is a must in order to impart not only potential and practical knowledge but also to exhibit in depth picture of successful

ventures. Besides, at institutional level necessary training should also be catered.

3. At each Taluk level deserving candidates list should be prepared in consultation with all the co-ordinators of entrepreneurial cell of the various institutions and for those members, in their interested area specific entrepreneurial training should be given for the promotion and improvement of practical knowledge.
4. The various Taluk level heads must be under one corporate body control. This corporate body must be like a Quasi-Government.
5. Another main duty of the above mentioned corporate body should be preparation of project plan for the different nature of industries for different sizes, even for the micro-enterpriser which will facilitates the new entrepreneurs in order to perceive ideas concretely for starting of new enterprises.

American system of true enterprise has always engendered the spirit of entrepreneurship. United States became a world economic power through entrepreneurial activity. Future rests squarely on entrepreneurial ventures founded by creative individuals not only in India but also in the world level. Entrepreneurship constitutes the driving force of the American dream. Why not in India also?

References

1. David H. Hold, *Entrepreneurship New Venture Creation.*
2. S. Saravanavel, *Entrepreneurial Development.*
3. Dr C.B. Gupta, and Dr. N.P. Srinivasan, *Entrepreneurship Development.*
4. (Government of India), *Economic Survey,* 2002-2001.

2

New Dimensions of An Entrepreneurship in 21st Century

*T. Ramasamy**

Economic development of a country depends on the growth of number of entrepreneurs. The large number of inventions would provide a basis for the growth of number of entrepreneurs. The inventions would have gone waste if no growth of entrepreneurs. In this way, inventions have to be commercialised by the entrepreneur. Modern technology is used to stand as a pioneer in the business world. So, initial task of an entrepreneur is change the invention into commercial practice.

In 1991, Government of India launched economic reforms. Dimensions of entrepreneurship was changed after economic reforms brought in India. It is a well known fact that India's real resource advantages are entrepreneurship, intellectual capital and knowledge workers. So, only the new dimensions of an entrepreneurship can adjust the changing situations in 21st century.

Current Affairs Knowledge

Entrepreneurs should know the latest happenings in the world. He can analyse the event regarding the impact of an

* T. Ramasamy, M. Com., M. Phil., PGDHRD PGDM., PGDMA, Department of Business Administration, Government Arts College, Paramakudi-623 707.

event on his business. Entrepreneurs will be isolated and wipe off from the business in the long run in the absence of knowledge on affairs. An effort on an entrepreneur is necessary to know and understand the current affairs. The following steps should be taken by the entrepreneur to have enrich on current affairs.

Collect reliable and authentic secondary data and information.

Read the data and information.

Interpret the data and information.

Analyse the impact in general.

Analyse the impact on his business line.

Read the feelings and the steps are taken by fellow entrepreneurs.

Draw the conclusion.

Frame the strategy.

The type of procedure can be followed by the entrepreneur. He can subscribe the magazines and journals to know current information and read them without any delay.

The strength of literacy is determining the strength of entrepreneurship. Literacy empowers entrepreneurs to stand on his legs. Proper documentation of collected data and information is done by the entrepreneur. The information can be supplied to the executives of an organisation whenever demanded and/or necessary. An ideal entrepreneur can add new dimensions into the existing dimensions by acquiring knowledge on current affairs.

Linkage with Association

A should be created with the help of single hand. There is a need of two hands to create a sound. If more number of hands joined together, the volume of sound will be high. According to this concept, an entrepreneur should be a member of an association. Under barter economy system, there is no need of association and membership. Now, it is a time of globalisation era. Hence, there is a need of an association and membership to survive in the business.

Entrepreneur has to create an opportunity or a platform to discuss about the functioning of a business. A healthy debate is welcome in the association to know the changing dimension of the business. In the fast developing internet world, there is a possibility of changing in the dimension of the business in every second. A change in the dimension of business leads to a change in the dimensions of entrepreneurship. Here, an entrepreneur is not only concentrate on his business but also watch on the movement of an association.

An exchange of views, opinions and/or ideas is possible whenever an entrepreneur has close contact with association activities. He can understand others and others can understand him too. Mutual understanding among entrepreneurs is facilitating the understanding and enrichment of emerged new dimensions in the days to come. An entrepreneur should be an instrumental in character to motivate others and being a model to others. Such type of entrepreneurs is accepted by any body.

Relationship with Government

Industrial policy of government plays a vital role in the development of entrepreneurship. The policy of the government is changed over a period time or whenever a change in the policymakers of government. So, an entrepreneur should be well versed with the industrial policy of the government and have a smooth relationship with government.

Now, the planning commission offers for industry in the changing environment is mild endorsement of further liberalisation of imports, removal of reservations for small scale industrial units, flexible labour laws and reformed state administrations for 10 per cent industrial growth. A smooth relationship with government will boost the entrepreneurs for his development. If strained relationship is prevailing between government and entrepreneur, the ultimate loser will be entrepreneur. Achievement of targets or objectives by maintaining smooth relationship is an intellectual activity.

This type of intelligent activity frees the entrepreneur from many ways like no mental stress some, tax concessions, avail credit facility, investment subsidy etc.

Relationship with Customers

In a world of heightened, competition, entrepreneur has to decide the type of relationship maintained with the customer. Customer data bank can be created and used for improving or maintaining better relationship with the customer. Better relationship with the customer is based on the leadership style of the entrepreneur, dealings and approach of sales executives with customers and adoption of strong customer focus across the organisation.

Customer is king in business—olden days concept. Now, this concept has been changed into customer is a friend. So, there must be close interaction with customer. Entrepreneur should take an interest on customers. Says Das Narayandas, Associate Professor at the Harvard Business School, "When you want to get down to managing customers, a good step to start with is the management of interactions." Entrepreneur can classify customers as satisfied customers and dissatisfied customers. A different strategy is adopted to maintain relationship with satisfied customers and dissatisfied customers separately. More lessons or valuable points are available from the dissatisfied customers than satisfied customers. All the points should be taken into consideration by the entrepreneur to attract new customers and retain old customers. Customers can also be classified on satisfaction levels. Higher the satisfaction, greater is the expected loyalty. Likewise, higher the dissatisfaction, greater the expected disloyalty or move from the company. So, an entrepreneur has to focus on customers than on products.

Relationship with Employees

Thoughts of an entrepreneur are visualised by the employees. A dot of an entrepreneur is to be converted into a picture by the employees. There must be a cordial relationship with employees. If an entrepreneur apply perfume in the hands of employees, in turn, employees are also applying perfume in the hands of entrepreneur, when both entrepreneur and employees are smelling perfume. If not so, both are benefited nothing. Hence, it is the duty of an entrepreneur to have a cordial relationship with employees.

Employees are facing two types of problem while performing a work. First type of problem is connected with the nature of work. Second type of problem is connected with the personal life. If there is any stress in the minds of an employee, the quality of performance is very less. So, the stress of an employee can be eliminated or reduced by an entrepreneur. Counselling can be introduced in an organisation and ideas are to be sold in the counselling centre to solve the problems of an employee by themselves.

An entrepreneur must create opportunities for upliftment of employees. Every employee wants to be promoted over a period of time. If an entrepreneur adopt a policy of promotion is based on efficiency. He can arrange facilities to improve the efficiency of employees. This type of relationship brings more benefits to an entrepreneur in the long run.

An entrepreneur has exercise two role while maintaining relationship with employees. First role is an employer. The second role is a good friend. As an employer, work has been assigned on the basis of ability and knowledge of work and paying reasonable wage to the employee. As a good friend, highlight the efficiency and special features of an employee and don't disclose the matters which are detrimental to the image of an employee. The quality of work performed by an employee is improved with the degree of encouragement available from the entrepreneur. Oral encouragement is also leads to better relationship with employees. There is no additional expenses to entrepreneur if he adopts oral encouragement. Monetary encouragement is to be followed on need basis. Better relationship with the employees leads the business into next generation.

Social Accountability

Entrepreneur has a social accountability of supplying quality goods in the hands of society. Total quality Management is the buzzword in the last decade of 20th century. Now, Total Value Management is the new buzzword. Total value means fulfilling the changing needs of the society at the earliest. Total value management will sustain the consistent creation of superior value to customers and simultaneously trigger superior value to various groups of stakeholders—share holders, employees, suppliers and others.

Entrepreneur should take initiative steps to provide better service to the society. Whatever the product is produced by the entrepreneur, the concerned product must deliver more and more benefits to the society. There is no harmful to the society in health point of view. The wastages of the product does not bring any inconvenience to the society. In other words, the wastages should be disposed of by the entrepreneur and give respect to air pollution. The bahaviour of an entrepreneur results not only entrepreneurial development but also development of a country.

Latest Entrepreneurship Styles

Under the globalisation climate, the entrepreneur is going to change his dimensions from time to time. So, there is a need of some latest entrepreneurship styles to the entrepreneur in order to design the dimensions perfectly. Here, some of the latest entrepreneurship styles are presented.

1. *Walking Faster than Employees*

   An entrepreneur should have more knowledge of business than his employees.

2. *Face to Face Talk*

   A discussion or consultation brings a new idea to both entrepreneur and employee.

3. *Writing on Post*

   Forgotten can be eliminated by writing in pocket diary and request assistant and/or employees to remember.

4. *A Solution to a Question*

   Entrepreneur can request the assistant and/or employees to frame the strategy to achieve the objectives within certain norms.

5. ***Having no Knowledge***

   Entrepreneur can empower the employees without managing the employees but exercise control on them.

6. ***Creative Thinking***

   Entrepreneur can motivate their employees for creative thinking.

7. ***Open Door***

   Complete freedom is given to employees on arrival and departure but demand 100 per cent achievement.

8. ***Speak with Smile***

   The information supplied by an entrepreneur can reach all employees within 15 minutes.

9. ***Education for All***

   Entrepreneur should educate all employees to avoid clues and lazy.

10. ***Use of Buzz Words***

    Code words can be used for quick dissemination of information. Secrecy is also maintained.

REFERENCES

1. Dr. Poonam Sharma and Vijaya Lakshmi *"Women Entrepreneurs and Finance"*, Social Welfare May 2002, Vol. 49 No: 2, pp. 19-24.
2. A.P. Sebastian Titus, *"Promotion of Women Entrepreneur Through Self Help Groups"*, Khadi Gramodyog, Nov. 2002 Vol. XXXXIX No: 2 pp. 68-72.
3. N.J. Jhaveri, *"Industry must Assume Leadership in Reforms"*, Economic and Political Weekly, January 18, 2002 Vol. XXXVIII No: 3 pp. 195-203.
4. Jose Paul, N. Ajith Kumar and Paul T. Mampilly, *"Entrepreneurship Development"* Himalaya Publishing House, Mumbai, Reprint 1999.
5. Dr. C.B. Gupta and Dr. N.P. Srinivasan, *"Entrepreneurship Development in India"*, Sultan Chand and Sons, New Delhi, Reprint 1998.
6. B.N. Neelima and T. Shyam Swaroop, *"Training Women for Entrepreneurship"* Social Welfare July 2000 Vol. 47 No: 4 pp 3-6.
7. Arundhuti Dasgupta, *"Playing the Right Cards in CRM"* Indian Management, February 2003, Vol. 42 Issue 2 pp. 23-27.

3

Entrepreneurship Management—Its Role in IT

*Dr. A. Venkatachalam**

*A. Jeyapragash***

Introduction

In the present LPG day, geographical coverage of market for products and services is ever increasing. It helps the business houses to carry out its commercial activities like marketing, selling, delivering, servicing and paying for products and services through Electronic Commerce. Now-a-days small business concerns can reach the global market as multinational companies have done. This global reach forces the marketers to think in new ways. For instance, products produced at some remote village will have an easy access to the international market.

IT refers to the paperless exchange of business information using network-based technologies. It may be defined as "Business anywhere around the world and at any time". In the past a consumer had ample time to go from store to store, locate the desired item, bargain, place order and finally get the supply. This entire process could range from a few hours to weeks depending on the product, quantity, quality and source of purchase. But the entire scenario has

* Dr. A. Venkatachalam, M. Com., M. Phil., B. Ed., Ph. D., PGDCA., Reader in Commerce, G.T.N. Arts College, Dindigul (Tamil Nadu).

** A. Jeyapragash, M. Com. M. Phil. PGDCM Lecturer (SG) in Commerce, G.T.N. Arts College, Dindigul.

changed. We are in the world of electronic, i.e. EDI (Electronic Data Interchange), EFT (Electronic Funds Transfer), E-cash (Electronic Cash), E-stamp (Electronic Stamp), E-mail (Electronic Mail) or E-commerce (Electronic Commerce).

Role of Entrepreneurship in Economic Development

Industrial development is the backbone for the economic development and industrial development envisages entrepreneurial development, i.e., entrepreneurial development leading to industrial development and the later leading to economic development and so the emphasis on entrepreneurial development.

Effectiveness of small enterprises depends upon the entrepreneurial and managerial capabilities of those involved in the business. Further they require information, which should be quickly analysed and effectively implemented. Entrepreneurs create new markets and facilitate expansion into international markets. It can be achieved by the entrepreneurs with the help of information technology.

Role of IT in Entrepreneurship Management

IT plays a dominant role in the areas of applications of business-to-consumer, business-to-business, and internal business processes.

1. ***Business-to-Consumer***

IT, between business and consumers, is accelerating the impact of information technology on consumer behaviour and business processes and markets. It establishes the interrelationships among electronic IT, consumer behaviour, and business processes and competition. So, the wide-open economic model of the Internet and the fast pace of change in Internet technologies are fundamental contributors to the development of Electronic Commerce applications between business and consumers. Retailing on the Web is an example for the same.

2. ***Business-to-Business***

Business-to-Business Electronic Commerce is the wholesale side of the commercial process. For example, if a business house wants to produce and sell a product to other business houses, it must purchase raw material and a variety of contract services from other business houses in order to produce and sell a product. These activities constitute the work of business relationships. For example, Intel sells its chips to other business organisations.

3. *Internal Business Process*

The purpose behind intra organisational IT is to help a business houses to maintain relationships. This is essential to ensure superior customer service. Many business houses like software companies are customer driven and market driven. Therefore constant monitoring and evaluation of data regarding customers, suppliers, and competitors should be compiled from their web sites and discussion groups. The feed back obtained is used to shape the organisation strategies in terms of product design, advertising, customer services etc. IT facilitates managers to communicate using video conferencing, e-mail and bulletin boards so that information is better disseminated and right decisions can be made.

Today large corporate Intranets have been installed so that information can be assessed and published. Online publishing helps to reduce costs related to printing and distributing. Faster delivery of current information takes place. Since information travels faster there is a better co-ordination between the various departments. In fact all efforts are being made to convert organisations into a paper less office.

Business Value of the IT

IT helps a business house overcome geographic constraints, time, cost, and structural barriers. These four capabilities emphasis how several applications of IT can help a firm capture and provide information quickly to end users at remote geographic locations at reduced costs as well as support its strategic organisational objectives.

1. *Overcoming Geographic Barriers*

IT gives an opportunity to the business houses to capture information about business transactions from remote locations or from anywhere in the world. It also provides better customer service by reducing delay in filling orders and improves cash flow by speeding up the filling of customers.

2. *Overcoming Time Barriers*

IT helps business houses to provide information to the needy persons immediately after it is requested. For example, credit inquiries can be made and answered in seconds.

3. *Overcoming Cost Barriers*

IT reduces the cost of more traditional means of communications. The new technology reduces expensive business trips, allows customers, suppliers, and employees to collaborate and improves the customer services. For example, business houses can now access the world through phone at a highly subsidised rate.

4. *Overcoming Structural Barriers*

IT establishes strategic relationship with their customers and suppliers by making the exchange of electronic business documents like order form, quotations in voice, and others fast, convenient and tailored to the needs of the business people involved.

These capabilities allow business houses to generate cost savings from using Internet, an ensure better customer service and relationship through interactive marketing.

Interactive Marketing

IT may also be used to enable a multi level action between a company's marketing, development, and customer support personnel, and its customers and prospective customer. The goal of interactive marketing is to attract and keep customers with a business in creating, purchasing and improving products and services. Customers are no longer just passive participants, who receive media advertising prior to purchase. Instead, they are actively engaged in a network-enabled proactive and, Interactive marketing experience. The various steps of the interceptive marketing process on the Internet are given below:

1. *Segment and Identify Potential Customers*

Initial market research done by reaching relevant groups-www servers, new groups.

2. *Create Promotional, Advertising and Education Material*

WWW page with multimedia streets-Audio and Video product information and complementary products, order forms and questionnaires.

3. *Put the Material on Customers Computer Screens*

Push-based marketing-Direct marketing using web broad casters, new groups and E-mail pull-based marketing-Indirect (static) marketing-www page.

4. *Interacting with Customers*

Dialogue with the customers. Interactive discussion among customers about various features offering endorsements, testimonials, questions/answers.

5. *Learning from Customers*

Incorporating feedback from customers in advertising, marketing strategy. Identifying new markets, using experience in new product development.

6. *Online Customer Service*

Fast, Friendly, solutions to customer problems.

For example, as a prospective customer, you might surf the web until you find a web site with products or a message that interests you. Then you might randomly view hyper media information about the company and its products and services. Next, you might hot link to a company-sponsored discussion forum, a Usenet newsgroup that discusses similar products and engage in online discussions.

At this point, you might switch to a competing web site via a URL or hot button provided by the newsgroup or an Internet search engine. Then you might send and receive e-mail messages about a particular product from marketing representatives of its vendor on the web. All this activity occurs prior to your online credit check and purchase process.

Finally, as a new customer, you may share questions, compliments, compliments and suggestions for improvement of the product via a web questionnaire, e-mail or a discussion group interaction with the vendor's customer support specialists.

Conclusion

Our country is known for its richness in natural resources. If we utilise the resources judiciously, per capita income will increase considerably. It provides an abundant opportunity to market our rural products to the nook and corner of the world. We require trained manpower to handle IT. Our government must take necessary steps to create awareness about IT in the minds of entrepreneurs, so that we will be prosperous.

4

Promotion of Women Entrepreneurship through Self-help Groups

*Dr. L. Rengarajan**

Rabindra Nath Tagore has rightly said, "Woman is the builder and moulder of the nation's destiny. Though delicate and soft as a lily, she has a heart for stranger and bolder than man. She is the supreme inspiration for man's onward march, an embodiment of love, pity and compassion".

Need for Promotion of Women Entrepreneurs

Women are the most efficient route to end hunger and poverty, as seven out of ten of the world's poor are women, with about 550 million living below poverty line. As per 1991 census work participation rate of women is 22 per cent. These statistics reveal that women, require the special attention of the development activities and there is urgent need for the promotion of women entrepreneurs.

Entrepreneurship is a more suitable profession for women than regular employment in public and private sectors since they have to fulfill dual roles.

In the last ten years the women of India have taken the bold step of invading the hitherto forbidden land of

---

* Dr. L. Rengarajan, Reader in Commerce, Rajapalayam Rajus' College, Rajapalayam, (Tamil Nadu).

entrepreneurship, the enduring bastion of male dominance. They are ready to prove to the world that their role in society is no more limited to that of buyers but can extend to that of successful sellers.

The World Bank Report and the 4th world conference on women declared that women are central to the success of poverty alleviation efforts—hence the importance of women's empowerment and their full participation on the basis of equality in all spheres of society. Studies reveal that money earned by poor women is more likely to be spent on the basic needs of the family than earnings generated by men.

Education for women should give importance to income earning activities. The process of learning by doing and earning would certainly empower women. More and more women need to be involved in self-employment. Self-employment is also conductive to the development of individual initiative and entrepreneurial talent and offers greater personal freedom.

Self-help Groups

The emergence of self-help group is a welcome development for empowerment of women. A self-help group (SHG) is a group of about 20 people from a homogeneous class, who come together for addressing their common problems. They are encouraged to make voluntary thrift on a regular basis. They use this pooled resource to provide small interest bearing loans to their members. The process helps them imbibe the essentials of financial intermediation including prioritisation of needs, setting terms and conditions and accounts keeping. This gradually builds financial discipline in all of them. They also learn to handle resources of a size that is much beyond their individual capacities. This mature financial behaviour encourages banks to make loans to the SHG in certain multiples of the accumulated savings of the SHG. The bank loans are given without any collateral and at market interest rates. The groups continue to decide the terms of loans to their own members. Since the group's own accumulated savings are part and parcel of the aggregate loans made by the groups to their members, peer pressure ensures timely repayments.

Therefore, the Government and NGO's have thought it fit encourage women to start micro-enterprises. The micro-enterprises are sought to be promoted by the SHGs. SHGs have come to say as the reliable forum for savings and credit. Rural women perform better by overcoming their timidity and inhibitions when they form themselves into groups. They have shown that they are creditworthy and can handle money responsibility and work as teams. The Governments and the NGO's all over the world found these groups viable for the promotion of women entrepreneurship.

The Government of India intends to provide a large portion of credit under the programme Swarnajayanthi Gram Swarozgar Yojana (SGSY) to SHGs for promoting micro enterprises. Each group is eligible to get about three lakhs rupees under the scheme with subsidy and infra-structural provisions. The Small Industries Development Bank of India, NABARD, Tamil Nadu Women's Development Corporation (TWDC) and District Rural Development Agencies extend financial support and training facilities aimed at capacity building of rural women. It has been estimated that there are five lakh women entrepreneurs in Tamil Nadu, promoted by TWDC over a period of five years.

Models of Self-help Group-Bank Linkage

There are three different models of credit linkage. SHGs formed and financed by banks, SHGs formed by NGOs and formal agencies but directly financed by banks, and SHGs financed by banks using NGOs and other agencies as financial intermediaries.

Model I: SHGs formed and Financed by banks. In this model, banks themselves take up the work of forming the groups, opening their saving accounts and providing them bank loans. By March 2002, 16 per cent of the total number of SHGs financed were from this category.

Model II: SHGs formed by NGOs and formal agencies but directly financed by banks. This model continues to have the major share, with 75 per cent of the total number of SHGs financed by 2002 falling under this category. Here NGOs and formal agencies in the field of microfinance act only as facilitator. They facilitate organisation and formation of groups, and train them in thrift and credit management. Banks give loans directly to these SHGs.

Model III: SHGs financed by banks using NGOs and other agencies as financial intermediaries. This is the model where the NGOs take on the additional role of financial intermediation. In areas where the formal banking system faces constraints, the NGOs are encouraged to approach a suitable bank for bulk loan assistance. This, in turn, is used by the NGO for lending to the SHGs.

In areas where a very large number of SHGs have been financed by bank branches, intermediate agencies like federations of SHGs are coming up as links between bank branch and member SHGs. These federations are financed by banks, which, in turn, finance their member SHGs. Other agencies like NBFCs are also coming up to take up this role.

The share of cumulative number of SHGs linked under this model up to March 2002 continues to be relatively small at 9 per cent but in years to come, this is expected to become a major delivery mode.

Progress of SHGs in India

SHG-Bank Linkage Programme Cumulative Progress (March 31, 2002)

Upto end of March	*Number of SHGs financed by Bank*	*Bank loans (Rs. Million)*	*Refinance from NABARD (Rs. Million)*
1999	32,995	571	521
2000	114,775	1,930	1,501
2001	263,825	4,809	4,007
2002	461,478	10,263	7,965

It could be observed from the above table that there is tremendous increase in the number of SHGs financed by banks from 32,995 as on March 1999 to 4,61,478 by the end of March 2002. The cumulative figure of total bank loans granted has increased from Rs. 571 million as on March 1999 to Rs. 10,263 million as on March 2002.

These 461,478 SHGs financed by banks were instrumental in extending the reach of bank finance to 7.8 million poor families comprising an estimated 39 million poor people. NABARD, through its micro finance programme, aims to provide banking services to 100 million poor, through one million SHGs by 2008.

SHGs have helped micro-enterprises by women individually and as groups. The newspapers frequently reported successful such endeavours in the recent years. The examples are raising vegetables in the land commonly owned, ready-made garment making, developing model farms-integrating agriculture, horticulture and animal husbandry, cultivation of medicinal herbs, mushroom cultivation, pot making, stone quarrying, sheep breeding and marketing wool, preparation of pickles, running canteens in Government Office premises, taking on lease coconut groves, making sheet metal products, running a minibus, setting up mechanised dry cleaning centres, running public distribution outlets and so on.

Some important details on self-help groups functioning in the southern districts of Tamil Nadu and their role in promotion of women entrepreneurship as appeared in the recent dailies are presented below.

Tiruchi District

There are 3688 Rural Self-help Groups functioning in Tiruchi District. The effective implementation of the Swarnajayanthi Gram Swarozgar Yojana (SGSY) has paved way for establishment of many micro-enterprises in rural areas of Tiruchi district by members of SHGs. These SHGs had established micro-enterprises of ready-made garment-making, gem-cutting, mushroom cultivation, handloom-weaving floriculture, greeting cards making, preparation of herbal medicines etc. in rural areas. Some groups have also successfully undertaken the job of stone chiseling, coir making, thatch-knitting etc. The SHG in Thuraiyur block established mushroom farms adopting scientific techniques able to earn a profit of Rs. 6000 a month. Programmes are conducted regularly for skill upgradation and entrepreneurship development to keep the SHGs active and fully involved.

Madurai District

Kottampatti Women Self-help Group

Most of the people in Kottampatti village are agricultural labourers, the absence of an economic crisis at Kottampatti is a clear evidence of the enormous role played by the women SHGs. Six women SHGs of Kottampatti began a business each at a newly constructed building in the village under the SGSY. These groups have identified the following businesses. Rice trade, sale of household utensils, rental service of large utensils for special festivals and ceremonies, footwear, coir ropes and manufacture of cement blocks with designs. These SHGs benefited from an Entrepreneurship Development Programme launched by the Social Welfare Department under the Mahalir Thittam. These women have been trained in all aspects of business such as maintaining accounts and how to approach bank officers for loans.

Kanyakumari District

The district administration and the District Rural Development Agency (DRDA) have identified the women from four self-help groups and arranged a ten-day training programme in producing plates and trays using the arecanut sheath. The plates and trays manufactured from arecanut sheath serve as an ideal substitute for plastic plates and trays. As they are made out of natural sheath the products are eco friendly and can be burned after use. The women were also trained in making paper cups, paper carry bags using paper pulp and a combination of either grass or dried leaves and flower petals. Cost wise these products are economical. Each tray or plate produced for ten paise could be sold for 30 paise, while the paper cup, carrying production cost of 30 paise could be sold for 50 paise.

Ramanathapuram District

There are 4000 self-help groups in this district with the total saving of Rs. 6 crores. The Government has allotted Rs. 2 crores for the construction of 218 SHG buildings in different parts of the district. Steps are taken to extend the area of sea weed cultivation from Mandapam to Devipattinam to create employment opportunities for fisher women. The Social Welfare Department conducts periodically work shops to sort out the problems in production, marketing and fixing prices for the SHG products.

Dindigul District

A women self-group in Dindigul district runs a unit providing agro, services with the total turnover crossing Rs. 12 lakhs per annum.

Theni District

The total savings of 2400 self-help groups in the Theni district has touched Rs. 4.6 crores. A revolving fund of Rs. 63.75 lakhs was disbursed to 255 SHGs under the Golden Jubilee Gram Self-Employment Scheme and an industrial loan of Rs. 1.53 crores to 10 SHGs. The SHGs are manufacturing note book, coir thread, foot rest, readymade garments, soaps and cultivating medicinal plants.

In a few Districts the Government has initiated a programme to establish sales centres to market the products produced by the SHG members

Conclusion

Though there are many hurdles involved in the process of promoting enterprises through Self-help Groups, the attempt is worthwhile one and the sustained efforts by the Government, NGOs and SHGs in the long run can generate a huge employment opportunities among the rural women and thus eradicate poverty among the rural masses.

5

Government Assistance and Rural Development Opportunities

*Dr. V.K. Somasundaram**

Standing on the threshold of 21st century, every one is quite aware of the ongoing process of liberalisation, privatisation and globalisation. As a result, opening up of our economy to the participation of the world has become inevitable and on the positive approach lot of opportunities and challenges has to be met and exploited. 80% of the village and small industries continue to grow and flourish. Even today 70% of the population of our country lives in rural areas. Agriculture and the allied activities is the mainstay of the rural India and in fact agriculture contributes about 35% of the country's GDP.

The development of rural industries has been one of the important elements of industrial policy of India. Progress of the rural sector has become sine quo non as it is closely associated with employment opportunities. However, the present socio-economic situation does not present much satisfactory state of affairs in spite of larger investment in these areas.

On the prospective side, the Indian economy has entered in the new millennium with some vigour and strength. India's

* Dr. V.K. Somasundaram, Head, Dept. of Corporate Secretaryship, Bharathidasan Government College for Women, Pondicherry-605003.

GDP was at 5.8% in 1980s and accelerated to around 6.5% on the eighth plan and the same tempo was maintained in the 9th plan period also.

Root Causes of Unemployment in India

Poor Literacy Rate: The educational deficiencies of our population have been long a drag on our growth potential. Conveniently forgetting the other side, we have always taken pride in the quality of our skilled personnel, scientists and software wizards. But the fact is that the general level of education of the bulk of our population has been extremely low. Adult literacy was only 18.3% in 1951 and only increased to 28.3% by 1960 and 34.3% by 1971. This was undoubtedly one of the reasons for our persistently low employment opportunity since independence. Most recent estimates by the National Sample Survey Organisation (NSSO) though show a literacy rate of 62% (in 1996-97) it is, in fact, quite a low literacy level.

Population Growth: The population growth for a long period remained stubbornly above 2%. At last it appears to be declining. Kerala has celebrated achievements in these areas and followed by Tamilnadu, Karnataka and Andhra Pradesh. The Central Government with the strong support of the states must take utmost care in controlling the booming population to take the nation towards the advanced economy.

Fiscal Deficit: When economic reform began, our country faced an exceptionally severe crisis in fiscal condition. Meanwhile, the fiscal position of the states including the better-administered ones has deteriorated drastically. A great deal of fiscal correction is the need of the hour to all the states. Unlike the Centre, the states are not allowed to borrow freely and as a result fiscal deficit mounts.

Poor Exploitation of Rural Resources: The rural India is bestowed with lot of potential resources, which are yet to be exploited. This resources sqeeze has direct implication on our ability to accelerate growth in agriculture. Faster agriculture growth and broad-based rural development will pave way for greater employment opportunity. To achieve employment potential, strategies should be evolved to expand the investment in irrigation, land development, soil and moisture conservation, agri-research, development of agriculture marketing facilities, maintenance of rural roads.

The basic investment in rural infrastructure can be viewed as a social problem but unfortunately the level of these expenditures has in fact declined. Much larger investments are also needed in health and education particularly in rural areas to bring our developments at respectable level.

Government Assistance

The volume of direct and indirect subsidies in our economic system has risen resulting in generation of more employment opportunities. Major subsidies of the Central are on fertilizers, food which amounted to Rs. 24,000 crores (1999-2000). On similar grounds, there are massive undercharging for higher education, for hospital services, railway transport, postal services etc. The state governments are burdened by massive subsidies though they are meant for upliftment of the rural people. Electric power is supplied to farmers at 10% to 20% of the cost of production in most states and free in few states.

Liberalisation of industrial licensing and opening up of industry for foreign investment was an important milestone and of course the first generation reforms in rural areas. For the betterment of rural sector and to remove the regional imbalances the Governments are keen in taking concerted efforts. The administrators are already in the mega processes of lending their helping hand through financial corporations. Loan arrangements in the form of Term loans, Hire purchasing and leasing, setting up of industrial, electronic estates, information technology parks, growth centers are mainly aimed at better employment opportunities. Every Government invariably promotes lot of backward area schemes. To encourage the public to be of self-oriented, total exemption of various taxes and subsidies on cost of pollution control machineries are provided. Innumerable support measures are taken by government to assist the rural artisans, cottage industries and small-scale industries in tiny sector. Government organisations specially promote various schemes for rural women entrepreneurs for their self-reliance.

Though there are number of pulling factors such as poor literacy state, thick population etc. Government's strenuous effort give an impetus and fruitful result in generating employment opportunities to the rural public.

6

Growth of Small Scale Industries in Rural India

*M. Prema Kumari**

In a developing economy like India, a significant contribution to economic development and general prosperity is possible through the development of entrepreneurship in small scale sector. The need is to exploit the latent entrepreneurial talents existing in all walks of life and sharpen them through constant endeavour.

Importance of Entrepreneurial Development in Small Scale Sector

The small scale sector which emerges as the middle sector of our business and industrial structure, contributes very significantly to the growth of the economy industrial decentralisation resulting in balanced regional development is possible through entrepreneurship development in this sector.

The SSIs were visualised as a remedy panacea for the country's problem, especially the generation of employment for a very large work force. SSI sector makes a significant contribution to output (GDP) of this country. We may note that right from the beginning SSI had contributed more than one third of the country's GDP, accounted for a larger portion

* M. Prema Kumari, Research Scholar (M. Phil) St. Joseph's College Trichy, Tamil Nadu.

of organised employment and also contributed to nearly 35 to 40 per cent of India's exports. The growth of Small Scale Sector has exceeded the growth of manufacturing sector. In 2001, manufacturing sector registered a growth of 5.3% whereas that of the small scale sector registered a growth of 8.1%.

In view of its importance the Government has been taking various measures from time to time in order to enhance the productivity, efficiency and competitiveness of the SSI sector. In pursuance of the comprehensive policy package announced last year, the major developments that have taken place in the SSI sector during 2001-2002 are

1. The Corpus fund set up under the Credit Guarantee Fund Scheme has been raised to Rs. 200 crore from Rs. 125 crore.
2. Credit Guarantee cover against an aggregate credit of Rs. 22.28 crore was provided till the end of December 2001.
3. 14 items were de-reserved on June 29, 2001 related to leather goods, shoes and toys.
4. A new scheme named Market Development Assistance Scheme was launched exclusively for the SSI sector.
5. Under the Cluster Development Programme, 4 UNIDO assisted projects have been commissioned during the year.

In this era of globalisation, for a country to survive its economy should have world class quality and competitive price for its products particularly those of industries.

This country has to sustain the Small Scale Sector if it were to maintain the higher tempo of industrialisation and if the country sets a growth rate of 11 per cent for the industrial sector, small scale industry sector will have to grow at more than 12 per cent. This can provide greater impetus to employment generation and also for reducing regional disparities, which are now causing considerable social tension.

Labour and capital productivity being measures of efficiency, the small scale sector showed an improvement in its productivity from Rs. 12,721 in 1991 to Rs. 22,014 in 1998. However capital productivity was higher in Small Scale Sector whereas it showed a lower labour productivity. The Small Scale Sector has both higher output-capital ratio and labour-capital ratio.

Reservation Policy

It should be noted that in the development of SSI sector in India reservation of items of production in the SSI sector became an important component of SSI Policy. The main argument of continuation of reservation policy is that it serves the desirable objective of increased production, export and employment generation. Data show that 28 per cent of the total production originated from the reserved items and 60 per cent of the exports of SSI sector comes form the reserved items.

The Small Scale industries Hire Purchase Corporation provides machinery on hire purchase basis to the Small Scale entrepreneurs. Financing agencies like SIDBI were established to provide the full requirements of credit.

The Government introduced from June 2002 a Credit Guarantee Scheme for the SSI sector with a "Corpus Fund of Rs. 125 crores to facilitate small entrepreneurs to avail credit up to a certain limit from banks without having to bother for collateral security. The Corpus Fund should be enhanced to Rs. 1000 crore keeping in view that the credit requirement of the SSI sector is estimated at Rs. 64000 crore during the Tenth Plan period.

As the SSI sector is facing a perennial sickness it is attributed more due to the poor quality of its products. The improvement in quality requires both technology and capital. Therefore calling for an upgradation of the skills of labour and entrepreneurs is also required.

Conclusion

As has been said that the small scale sector is essential

for the balanced regional development the managerial skill and other skills of the entrepreneurs should be fine-tuned in such a way that the interests of the small scale industries are not affected at any point of time. The weaknesses of these units should be exploited in the interest of the economy of the country.

7

SSI and Entrepreneurship—Concomitant to One Another

*M. Jai Ganesh**

Entrepreneurship—An Overview

The beginning of twenty first century witnessed a new world of economic opportunities. Thanks to information technology revolution that is underway, new frontiers of science are being breached every day. Indian economy is integrating with the rest of the world at lightening speed. The entrepreneur is a key figure in such a scenario. He spots new opportunities and capitalises on the same to set up new enterprises. In the process he not only creates wealth for himself but also contributes to national prosperity and creates job.

Schumpeter, an authority on the subject, defines entrepreneur as "one who starts an industry, undertakes risk, bears uncertainties and also performs the managerial functions of decision-making and co-ordination". According to him, entrepreneurship is one form of labour that tells rest of the labour what to do and sees to it that it gets done.

Entrepreneur is a highly respected word in the developed nations. It conjures up visions of active, purposeful men and

* M. Jai Ganesh, M. Phil Scholar, Department of Commerce, St. Joseph's College, Trichy-2, Tamil Nadu.

women accomplishing a wide variety of significant deeds. Their actions bridge the gap between plans and reality. The entrepreneur has been described as an individual who undertakes to organise, manage and assume the risk of running a factory, a business or an enterprise. He ventures out, considers change as a means of growth and is prepared to take calculated risks. Motivated by an urge to make success of him, the entrepreneur does not accept things as they are but challenges the situation.

Entrepreneurship plays a vital role in industrial development. The industrially developed countries like USA, Germany and Japan bear the evidence that an economy is an effect for which entrepreneurship is the cause. Entrepreneurship has now emerged as a profession.

Like other economic concepts, entrepreneurship has been a subject of much debate and discussions. It is an elusive concept. Hence, different authors define it differently. While some call entrepreneurship as 'risk-bearing', others view 'innovating' and yet others consider it 'thrill-seeking'.

Entrepreneurship has been realised as one of the most important input in the economic development of a country. Economic growth and industrialisation is the possible by-product of entrepreneurship.

Importance of SSI With Regard to Entrepreneurship

The potential of entrepreneurship as a vehicle to harness the talent, capacities and energies of people so as to create a vibrant economy has been increasingly recognised in most developing countries. In India too, the transformational power of entrepreneurship was recognised ever since the advent of independence. It has been almost half a century that the nation event ahead with several small-scale industrial programmes in order to create economic development. The success of these efforts had unfortunately not been satisfactory.

The development of small-scale industries contributes to the increase in per capita income, i.e., economic development in various ways. It generated immediate employment opportunities with relatively low capital/investment, promotes more equitable distribution of national income makes effective mobilisation of untapped capital and human skills and leads to dispersal of manufacturing activities all over the country, leading to growth of villages small towns and economically lagging regions.

In India, the small-scale sector enjoys the place of pride as the engine of growth; it has grown in volume from 16,000 units in 1950 to an estimated 21 lakh units by the end of 1999, providing direct and indirect employment to over 75% of the country's labour force. Items produced by the small-scale sector ranges from consumer goods to high precision items. The scope of enterprise has also become broad-based.

Approximately 40% of total exports from the country are from the small sector, which is quite an achievement considering the lack of funds available to these entrepreneurs. They are able to withstand strong competition from countries like Korea, China and Taiwan because of their quick reaction time. If anything has gone out fashion, a small entrepreneur loses no time in coming out with another, while the large industry is slower to react. Small sector is also doing better in exports because of their ability to execute small orders. They can provide large varieties in small volumes, while big industry keeps worrying about economies of scale. India is doing extremely well in export of handicrafts, gems and jewellery and ready-made garments. And it is no coincidence that small entrepreneurs chiefly dominate all the three sectors.

SSI's and Employment

Today we have a population of over 400 million people living below the economic poverty line. The situation for most these families have not seen much change in the last 50 odd years of planned economic development. Poverty and unemployment continue to pose major obstacle in the path of rural development.

Widespread unemployment is one of the biggest problems facing the country. The entrepreneurs are the catalysts for socio-economic change and small enterprises are the medium for that. Small industries are generally labour-intensive and therefore promise wider employment possibilities for the ever-expanding population of India. They are also suitable as a supplementary source of employment for Indian farmers who remain out of work during lean period of agriculture season. Small industries offer promising opportunities to educated unemployed in the urban areas to become self-employed gainfully.

SSI provides maximum employment next only to the agricultural sector. According to economic survey, 1998-99, "the total number of small scale units in the country in 1997-98 was 30.14 lakh compared to 28.57 lakh in 1996-97. Value of production of small-scale units in 1997-98 aggregated Rs. 465171 crore. The volume of employment in small-scale sector stood at 167.2 lakh as of end March 1998.

Self-employment is an assault on the problem of unemployment and under employment. A number of countries are facing increasing problems because of unemployment. Many countries are experiencing helplessness in coping with the problem of unemployment. Vocational training, which enhances the ability of a person to start and run a small business, can become a solution to this wide spreading problem.

Conclusion

Industrialisation is one of the important means to usher in an economic and social transformation in the developing economies. More so, when agriculture cannot sustain the burden of increasing population, it is the industry and services sector, which have to shoulder the responsibility of sustaining and accelerating the pace of economic development. Therefore industrialisation is indispensable for the survival and growth of an economy.

We know that small-scale enterprises mean the enterprises with less capital/investment and more labour absorption, less technology oriented, using local resources, catering to local/regional demands so on and so forth. Small enterprises are commonly known for, what is called, 'one man show' in which the same person performs various roles simultaneously as an owner, a capitalist, an organiser, a manger, a labourer and what not. He is termed as the entrepreneur. This means there are as many entrepreneurs as are small enterprises. Thus, small-scale enterprises and entrepreneurs are concomitant to each other. Say, small industries precedes entrepreneur and entrepreneur precedes small industries. We cannot think of entrepreneurs without small-scale industries as they always go together.

Therefore, India needs a whole new breed of new entrepreneurs and development of Small Scale Industries to capitalise on the unfolding opportunities and propel the country on the path of prosperity and self-reliance.

References

Books

1. S.S. Khanka, *Entrepreneurial Development,* 1999 edition, S. Chand and Co. Ltd; New Delhi.
2. K.K. Sen, *Rural Industrialisation In India,* Sultan Chand and Sons.
3. Sulakshan Mohan, *Making of An Entrepreneur,* 2000 edition, Indian Publishers Distributors, Delhi.
4. C.B. Gupta and N.P. Srinivasan, *Entrepreneurial Development,* 1992 edition, Sultan Chand and Sons.
5. Vasant Desai, *Management of A Small Scale Industry,* Himalaya Publishing House.

Journals

6. *Southern Economist,* July 15, 2002 volume.
7. *Southern Economist,* November 1, 2002 volume.
8. *Southern Economist,* January 1, 2003 volume.
9. *Southern Economist,* January 15, 2003 volume.
10. *Economic and Political Weekly,* December 28, 2002 volume.

8

Small Scale Industry on Creating Powerful Entrepreneurism in India

*Capt. R. Rajasekaran**

Introduction

Industrial Development of any region is the outcome of the purposeful human activity and entrepreneurial thrust. Entrepreneur is presently at the crest of popularity. In India large number of people one seeking entrepreneurship as a career option. Increasing number of unemployed youth are getting attracted to entrepreneurship and are planning to set up their own business ventures. Entrepreneurial development is considered as a vital factor for the development of the country. In a way, small and large-scale enterprises are two legs of Industrialisation process of a country. Hence, small-scale enterprises are found in existence in every country. Small enterprises have been fixed an important place in the framework of Indian Planning since beginning both for economic and ideological reasons.

Small-Scale Industry (SSI)

Small-scale Industry comprises of variety of undertakings. The definition of small-scale industry varies from one country to another and from one time to another in

* Capt. R. Rajasekaran, M. Com, M. Phil, Lecturer -SG. Department of Commerce. PSG College of Arts and Science. Coimbatore-641 014.

the same country depending upon the pattern and stage of Development, Government Policy and administration set up of the particular country. As a result, there are at least 50 different definitions of SSIs found and used in 75 countries. All these definitions either relate to capital or employment or both or any other criteria.

As per the Abid Hussain Committee's recommendations on Small-scale Industries, the Government of India has, in March 1997, raised the Investment ceiling to Rs. 3 crores for small-scale industries and Rs. 50 lakhs for tiny units. But now, (w.e.f 21.12.1999) an industrial undertaking in which the investment in Fixed Asset in Plant and Machinery whether held on ownership terms on lease or on Hire purchase does not exceed Rs. 10 million. For Small-scale Industries, the Planning Commission of India user terms "village of Small-Scale Industries" These include modern Small-scale Industry and the traditional cottage and household industries. This is depicted in the following chart:

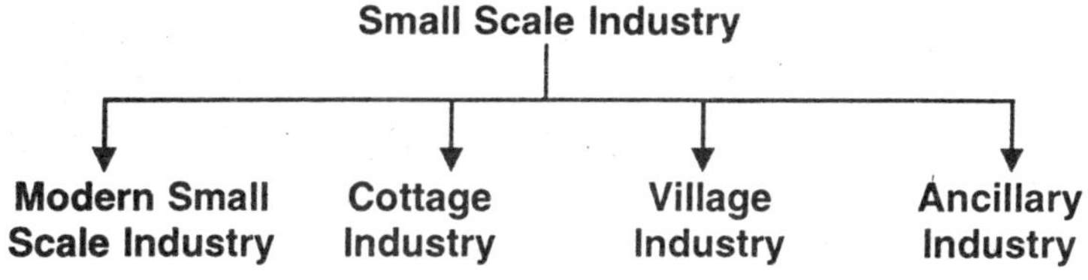

Types of Small-Scale Industries

Small-scale Industries can be classified into five main types as follows:

1. *Manufacturing Industries*

Industries producing complete articles for direct consumption and also processing Industries.

2. *Feeder Industries*

Specialising in certain types of products and services (e.g.) Costing, Electroplating, Welding etc.

3. *Serving Industries*

Covering light, repair shops necessary to maintain mechanical equipment.

4. *Ancillary to Large Industries*

Producing parts and components and rendering services.

5. *Mining or Quarrying*

Characteristics of SSI

"Small-scale Industry is beautiful" because of its following important characteristics:

- A small-scale unit is generally a one-man show. Even the small units, which run by a partnership firm or company, the activities are mainly carried out by one of the partners or directors. In practice, the others are simply as sleeping partners or directors who mainly assist in providing funds.
- In case of small-scale industries, the owner himself/herself is a manager also. Thus, these units are managed in a personalised fashion. The owner has first hand knowledge of what is actually going on in the business. He takes effective participation in all matter of business decision making.
- Composed to large units, a small-scale industrial unit has a lesser gestation period, i.e. the period after which the return on investment starts.
- The scope of operation of small industrial undertakings is generally localised catering to the local and regional demands.
- Small units use indigenous resources and therefore, can be located anywhere subject to the availability of these resources like raw materials, labour etc.
- Small Industries are fairly labour intensive with comparatively smaller capital investment than the larger units. Let the facts speak, according to P.C. Maholnobis, small scale units require very little capital but at the same time ten or fifteen times greater in comparison with corresponding factory system.
- Using local resources, small units are decentralised and dispersed to rural areas. Thus, the development

of small-scale industries in rural areas promotes more balanced regional development, on the one hand and presents the influx of job seekers from rural areas to cities and urbanising centres, on the other.

- Compared to large-scale units, small-scale units are more change susceptible and highly receptive socio-economic conditions. They are more flexible to adapt changes like Introduction of new products, New method of production, New materials and new markets, New forms of organisations etc.

Role of SSI and Entrepreneurial Development

The development of SSI contributes to the increases in per capita income i.e. economic development in various ways. It generates immediate employment opportunities with relatively low capital/investment, promotes more equitable distribution of national income makes effective mobilisation of untapped capital and human skills and leads to dispersal of manufacturing activities all over the country, leading to growth of villages, small towns and economically lagging regions. This promotes to balanced regional development.

Increasing number of persons of small enterprise means increasing number of person assuming the entrepreneur career has exactly, become *sine quo non* with increase in the number of small-scale enterprises. In pursuant of the Government of India's new small scale enterprise policy titled policy measures for promoting and strengthening small, tiny and village entrepreneurs tabled in the parliament on 6th August 1991 and later passed, the small sector is sure to develop and expand in coming years also. It infers to inter alia more chances for enterprising persons to assume the entrepreneurial career in future. Thus, small-scale enterprises serve as seeded for the emergence of entrepreneurship in the country.

Opportunities for Entrepreneurs in SSI

Small industry sector has performed exceedingly well and enabled our country to achieve a wide measure of industrial growth and diversification.

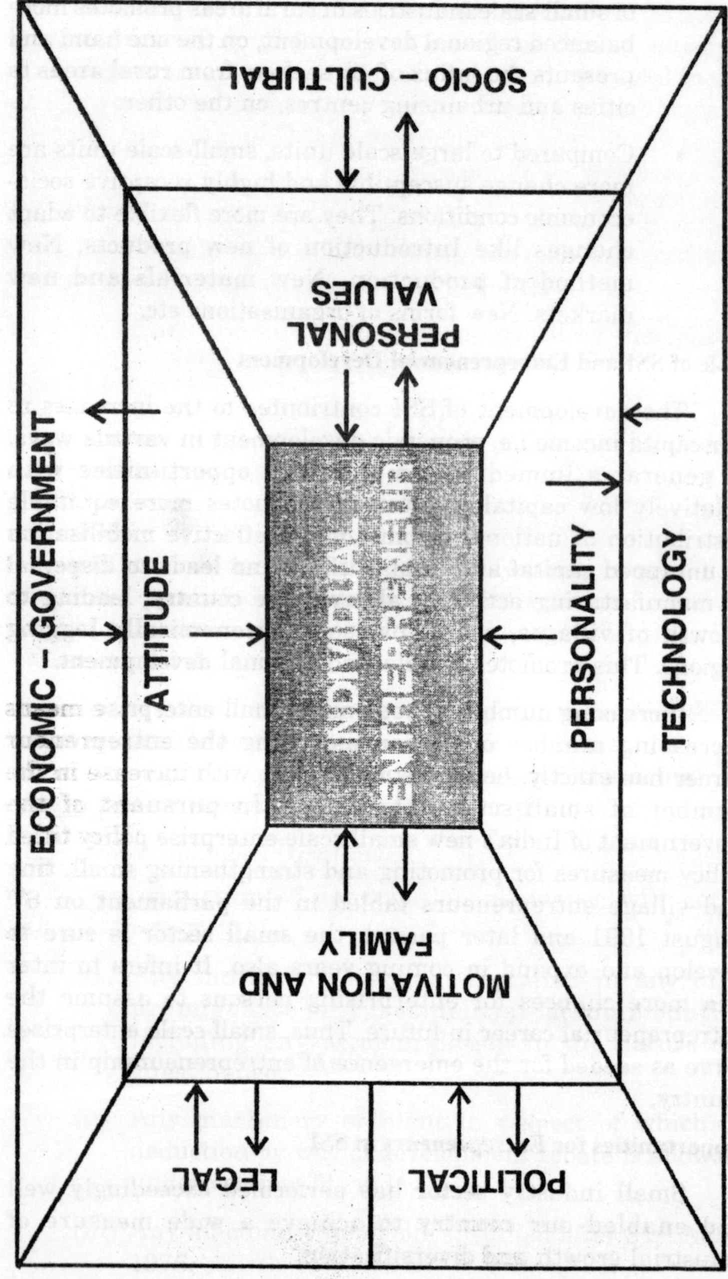
SOCIO – CULTURAL
PERSONAL VALUES
ECONOMIC – GOVERNMENT
ATTITUDE
INDIVIDUAL ENTREPRENEUR
PERSONALITY
TECHNOLOGY
MOTIVATION AND FAMILY
LEGAL
POLITICAL

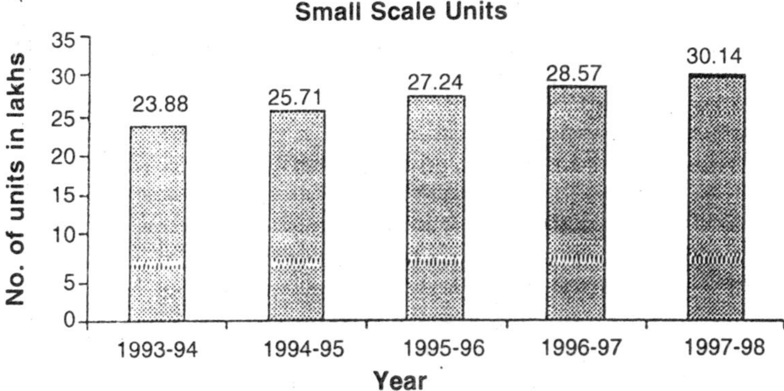

By its less capital intensive and high labour absorption nature, SSI sector has made significant contributions to employment generation and also to rural industrialisation. This sector is ideally suited to build on the strengths of our traditional skills and knowledge, by infusion of technologies, capital and Innovative marketing practices.

The opportunities in the small scale sector are enormous due to the following Factors:

- Less Capital Intensive
- Extensive Promotion and Support by the Government
- Reservation for Exclusive Manufacture by small scale sector
- Project Profiles
- Funding
- Finance and Subsidies
- Machinery Procurement
- Raw Material Procurement
- Manpower Training
- Technical and Managerial Skills
- Tools and Tools Utilisation Support
- Reservation for Exclusive Purchase by Government

- Export Promotion
- Growth in demand in the domestic market size due to overall economic growth
- Increasing Export Potential for Indian products
- Growth in Requirements for ancillary units due to the increase in number of greenfield, units coming up in the large scale sector.

So this is the opportune time to set up projects in the small-scale sector. It may be said that the outlook is positive, indeed promising, given some safeguards. This expectation is based on an essential feature of the Indian industry and the demand structures. The diversity in production systems and demand structures will ensure long term co-existence of many layers of demand for consumer products/technologies/ processes. There will be flourishing and well grounded markets for the same product/process, differentiated by quality, value added and sophistication. This characteristic of the Indian economy will allow complementary existence for various diverse types of units.

The promotional and protective policies of the Government have ensured the presence of this sector in an astonishing range of products, particularly in consumer goods. However, the bugbear of the sector has been the inadequacies in capital, technology and marketing. The process of liberalisation will therefore, attract the infusion of just these things in the sector.

Institutional Support to Entrepreneurs

Finance is one of the essential requirements of any enterprise. Before actually setting up their units, small entrepreneurs need to know very clearly about the type and extend of their financial requirements. The following institutions are providing financial assistance to those entrepreneurs.

- Commercial Banks
- Industrial Development Bank of India (IDBI)

- Industrial Finance Corporation of India (IFCI)
- Industrial Credit and Investment Corporation of India (ICICI)
- Industrial Reconstruction Bank of India (IRBI)
- Life Insurance Corporation of India (LIC)
- Unit Trust of India (UTI)
- State Finance Corporations (SFC)
- State Industrial Development Corporation (SIDCS)
- Small Industries Development Bank of India (SIDBI)
- Export-import Bank of India

There are many central and state government institutions are coming forward to help small entrepreneurs to establish and run the industry more effectively. These central and state government institutions are as follows:

- National Small Industries Corporation Limited (NSIC)
- Small Industries Development Organisation (SIDO)
- Small-scale Industries Board (SSIB)
- State Small Industries Development Corporations (SSIDC)
- Small Industries Service Institutes (SISI)
- District Industries Centre (DIC)
- Industrial Estates
- Specialised Institutes

The common services rendered by the above institutions are:

- Technology Consultancy
- Industrial Management Training

- Entrepreneurial Development Programme Scheme
- Ancillary Developments/Sub-Contract Exchange
- Marketing Assistance
- Export Promotion Marketing
- Modernisation/Upgradation Technology
- Assistance to Rehabilitation of sick units
- Common Facility and Training
- Assistance to District Industries Central/State Government/various Developmental Agencies in the State
- Technical Assistance to various Central Government Agencies like Director General of Foreign Trade, National Small Industries Corporation, Central Excise, Bureau of Indian Standards, CSIR etc.
- Exhibition/Demonstration.

Problems of Entrepreneurs in SSI

Though we have distinguished peculiarities for entrepreneur in SSI, we have found that the organisational pattern of these industries places them at a distinct disadvantage vis-à-vis the large sectors. Following problems are commonly faced by the entrepreneur, these are as follows:

- Problems of Raw material
- Problems of Finance
- Problems of Marketing
- Problems of Under-utilisation
- Problems of Labour force
- Problems of Government policy
- Problems of Technological obsolescence
- Problems of Inadequate supply of power
- Problems of Unorganised market channel
- Problems of Imperfect knowledge

Conclusion

Entrepreneurship in SSI as a distinct factor of production contributes to the economic development of a country. The wide range of significant contributions that entrepreneurship in SSI makes to the economic development include promotion of capital formation, creation of immediate employment, promotion of balanced regional development, effective mobilisation of capital and skill, induction of backward and forward linkages, etc.

Small-scale Industries encompass vast scope covering activities like manufacturing, servicing, retailing, financing, construction, infrastructure etc. In view of the Government of India's ever increasing importance given to the SSI in national economy, more and more small industries and more and more entrepreneurs are going to enter in future. Thus these are to provide ample opportunities to their people to assume bright entrepreneurial career.

References

1. M. Laxmi Narasaiah, *Development of Small-scale Industries.*
2. Vepa, *Small Industry Development Programme.*
3. A.R. Sen, *Small Industrial Loans*
4. S.C. Patra, *Promotion and Management of SSI.*
5. R.S. Jalal, *Industrial Entrepreneurship and SSI.*
6. D. Narendra Kumar, *Entrepreneurship in Small Scale Sector.*
7. S.S. Khanka, *Entrepreneurship Development.*
8. Jayshree Suresh, *Entrepreneurship Development.*
9. A. Shankaraiah, Rudra Saibaba and Ramana Rao Ponugoli, *Entrepreneurship Development,* Website www.ssiindia.com

9

Role of Commercial Banks in SSI's Entrepreneurship Development under Liberalisation Context

*Dr. S. Hasan Banu**

Introduction

Since Independence India has emphasised the need for promotion of informal and modern small enterprises so that this sector provides goods and services for mass consumption using labour-intensive technology. The strategy of encouraging small scale industries (SSI) can subserve multiple objectives like rapid increase in gainful employment, balance regional growth, mobilisation of the country's productive factors of production and entrepreneurial energies, checking the exodus of labour from rural to urban areas and sustaining industrialisation without disturbing ecological balance.

The Government of India (GOI) in order to accelerate the growth and productivity of SSI, has set up a number of promotional organisations/Boards/Commissions/Corporations etc. because of the comprehensive packages provided by the government and its various organisation significant growth of the micro enterprises, and SSI has taken place. In this context the paper presents the various availability of credit

* Dr. S. Hasan Banu, M. Com., M.Ed., M. Phil., Ph. D., Senior Scale, Dept. of Commerce, H.K.R.H. College, Uthamapalayam–625 533, Theni District.

from the public sector banks and problems associated with it and also make some suggestions for its sustainable growth in the liberalised and WTO environment.

Growth of SSI

Table 1
Growth of Small Scale Industries in India: 1980-81 to 1999-2000

Year	*No. of Units (in lakhs)*	*Output at Current Prices (Rs. Crores)*	*Employment (No. in Man-days) (in lakhs)*	*Export (at Current Prices) (Rs. Crores)*
1980-81	8.74	28,060	71.0	1,643
1990-91	19.38	1,55,340	124.3	9,100
1995-96	27.20	3,56,213	152.6	36,470
1996-97	28.57	4,12,636	160.0	39,249
1997-98	30.14	4,65,171	167.2	44,437
1998-99	31.21	5,27,515	171.6	49,481
1999-2000	32.25	5,78,470	178.0	53,975

Source: IBA Bulletin November 2001.

The above table shows the important structural changes that have taken place in the SSI sector in the post liberalised period is as follows.

- Production per unit has been increased from Rs. 8.58 lakh in 1991-92 to Rs. 18.07 lakh in 1999-2000.
- Production value per employee has increased from Rs. 1.38 lakh to Rs. 3.26 lakh
- Employment per unit was 6.23 in 1991-92 but it has declined to 5.55, which indicates that more capital intensive units had been set up post liberalised period.
- It is estimated that export which was Rs. 66,681 per unit in 1991-92 has increased to Rs. 1,76,173 in 1999-2000.

- While the share of SSI export in total export has marginally increased by 3.38 per cent between 1991-92 to 1999-2000.
- Of the total production 7.76 per cent was exported in 1991-92 as against 9.74 per cent in 1999-2000.
- The number of sick SSI units as percentage of total units has declined from 11.77 per cent in 1991-92 to 9.49 per cent in 1999-2000.

The above structural changes clearly indicate that this sector has inherent strengths and can prosper if proper policy inputs are provided in time. Even though the SSI enterprises have their own strength in practical they are facing more problems under WTO environment and liberalisation context.

Problems in the growth of micro enterprises and SSI

According to the 9th plan (1997-2001) the major problems faced in developing entrepreneurship in rural areas are

1. Inadequate flow of credit
2. Use of obsolete, technology machinery and equipment.
3. Poor quality standards
4. Inadequate infrastructure facilities.

In my paper I am going to stress the main two problems of inadequate flow of credit and use of obsolete technology, machinery and equipment, poor quality standard and role of banks in these areas to overcome these problems.

(a) Inadequate Flow of Credit

In our country, the banks provide assistance, for working capital, and fixed capital for inserting the industrial units.

One of the most important problems being experienced by the SSI sector relates to availability of adequate and timely credit both term loans and working capital. The data provided in Table 2 gives an idea about the flow of credit to SSIs during the post-liberalisation period (1989-90 to 2000-2001) by the public sector banks.

Table 2

Year Ending March	SSI Production	Net Bank Credit to SSI	Per cent of 3 to 2	Nayak Committee Actual Requirement		
				Working Capital (Actual)*	Minimum Credit Requirement**	Gap
1	2	3	4	5	6	7
1991	155340	16783	10.80	13090	31068	17978
1995	345776	25843	7.47	20157	69155	48998
1998	527515	38109	7.22	29725	105503	75778
1999	582732	48483	8.32	37816	116546	78370

*78 Per cent of total net bank credit to SSI. **20 per cent of column-2

Source: IBA Bulletin November 2001.

The data given in the table 2 shows that there is no relation between production in SSI and actual follow of credit. The above data also shows the big gap between the actual requirement and also actual credit flow to such unit. The percentage of actual credit to the minimum expected credit was 42% in 1990-91 which declined to 32 per cent in 1999-2000. *This clearly indicates that the majority of SSI depends on either unorganised money market or internal accrual for their working capital at high rate of interest.*

Timeliness of Credit

Even though the financial institutions have been providing term loans timely availability of working capital has been a continuing problem. Small entrepreneurs, particularly the first generation have been experiencing several hardships in obtaining timely sanction and disbursement of working capital. Banks seem to have an intrinsic distrust of such entrepreneurs and insist on collateral as a matter of routing even when the loan amounts are small and projects seen definitely viable.

The study sponsored in the post liberalised period by NIBM in 1994 indicated that the banks sanctioned 49.7 per cent of the number of applications within 3 months from the date of application. 22.9 per cent within 3 months to 6 months, 18-8 per cent between 6 to 12 months and 8-6 per cent beyond 12 months.

The situation as it emerges from the NIBM study is not so alarming as it generally made out to be although there exists scope for expeditious credit decision.

Sick of SSI Units

The small and medium enterprises as a group experience the problems related to credit, infrastructure, raw material, technology marketing brand name etc. all these problems lead to make the units non-performing or sick one.

Most of the SSI units at present are facing stiff competition because of the opening of the economy and WTO. Hence innovative schemes/programmes need to be evolved so that the SSIs are not only promoted but they can thrive on their own. In WTO environment, the banks, FIs will have to formulate a strategy to sustain the existing SSI units. For this purpose banks will have to formulate new financial products for

1. Technology upgradation
2. Quality of products
3. Marketing etc.

Suggestions

Moving away from pre-liberalisation era of protection, the small scale entrepreneur has been steadily reorienting themselves to face the challenges posed by an increasing competitive environment.

Modernisation and Technology Upgradation

In the liberalised environment, one factor that the small scale units have to keep in mind is the need for upgradation of technology in respect of their existing units and scouting for technology for setting up new units with a view to improving competitiveness of SSI units there is an urgent need for supporting modernisation and technology upgradation programmes.

The efforts of the banks in this regard should be directed towards.

- Creation of awareness about new technologies.
- Upgradation of technology and skill.
- Modernisation of obsolete technology.
- Energy conservation and
- Ancillarisation and subcontracting.
- Encourage the building up of quality culture among the small industries through designing financial assistance and programmes.
- Quality awareness programmes and credit camps should be organised for the benefit of the existing and prospective entrepreneurs.

- Liberal support for financing the setting up of in house testing and common testing facilities should be provided.
- Banks should ensure that purchases of raw materials by small enterprises are financed only if the materials quality standards are satisfied.
- Quality record should be the basis for additional assistance

The Emerging Personality of Small Scale Entrepreneur

The mere upgradation of technology alone will not enhance the quality of products. So there is a need for upgradation of skills, of the owner, manager, supervisors and skilled workers.

Small scale entrepreneurs, particularly the technocrat, the self-styled businessmen and small scale manufacture, symbolise the "Craftsman" (Smith-1967) narrow in education and training, low in social awareness and certain limitedness in dealing with the environment. This however, does not take away from them as "internal focus" that superscribes their character.

Marketing Strategy

Liberalisation has created threat as well as opportunities for this sector and this will have to be considered while provided marketing packages. There is a need to assist government agencies and public as well as private enterprises in respect of planning and development of marketing policies, strategies, facilities and techniques these include.

- Developing a body of local marketing specialists, consultants and researchers operating as marketing advisory boards at regional and state levels.
- Collecting, selecting and disseminating marketing information relating to all phases of planning and aspects of implementation of industrial projects and build up a marketing data bank for the use of national enterprises, institutions and government agencies.

- Encourage co-operation among local industries, institutions and educational bodies.
- Most of the new and existing entrepreneurs are unable to gather the required information due to paucity of skills, time, resources and required data.

The banks will have to play a major role in this regard.

Role of Banks in Providing Technology

The developments in Internet technology offer opportunities to reorganise the marketing infrastructure for the small and medium enterprises.

The worldwide web technology offer opportunities to reorganise the marketing infrastructure for the small and medium enterprises. The worldwide web technology offers a low cost, high technology outlet for advertising products and services to a wide ranging audience and a global market. The development of e-commerce on the other hand creates a low cost marketing mechanism.

So the role of the banking sector would also need to undergo change.

- Banks have acted as the providers of credit and custodian of financial assets of the business.
- Banks should act as the business partners of small enterprises by providing them e-commerce facilities and external information required by the small business.
- Banks would have to provide a lot of information on their websites about external events affecting the business as well as providing the information on economic activities of their small business.

The banks, therefore, would have to reinvent their role to support small-scale industry.

Conclusion

The policy packages for small scale and tiny enterprise announced by the Government of India are expected to promote not only technology, human resources development and identification of market places but also an adequate flow of finance for the proper functioning of small scale enterprises. Too much support in the form of subsidies and protection could jeopardize the efficient functioning of any enterprise. So banks should frame new innovative schemes and play an important role for the orderly growth of this sector.

10

The Role of Small Scale Industries for the Growth of Entrepreneurship in Dindigul District

*Dr. N. Markkandeyan**

*M. Ponnaiah***

Introduction

Development in Industry progresses steadily by providing greater employment potential in big Cities and Corporations due to infrastructural facilities. At the same time in the rural parts of India, industrial growth is not steady due to lack of infrastructure. Moreover rural people are more conservative about starting industries. In villages Labourers are migrating to Towns and Cities to get employment. This unbalanced growth of industries in the nation awakened the planners to plan for rural industrialisation. In order to stabilise the economic growth in the Villages through industrialisation and to prevent the migration of rural population to Towns and Corporations and also to start more industries in rural areas by providing subsidies and concessions the District Industries Centre (DIC) was formed throughout the nation.

* Dr. N. Markkandeyan, Reader in Commerce, G.T.N. Arts College, Dindigul, Tamil Nadu.

** M. Ponnaiah, Senior Lecturer in Commerce, G.T.N. Arts College, Dindigul.

The activities of DIC kindled a ray of hope in the hearts of the millions of villagers who aspired for better economic growth and raised their standard of living, which resulted in total upliftment of villages economically and socially. This concept gained momentum consequently on the formation of DIC.

Under the pretext of DIC, Government has announced support to the new industries by way of liberal financial support and subsidies etc. By availing these concessions, industries started growing steadily in rural areas. In addition to subsidies and concessions the Government has also simplified the licencing procedures and the DIC has been vested with powers to monitor even the approval of licences under single window concept meetings.

The promotion of small-scale industrial sector has become inevitable due to its inherent merits such as low capital intensity, short gestation period, high employment potential, capacity, to induce dispersal of industrial activities and widening of the entrepreneurial base-etc.

The liberalisation policy of 1991 however, had imposed a new challenge of competition of the S.S.I. units from large-scale industries, and multinational corporations. To make it competitive, the central government has been implementing a number of schemes for small-scale industries (SSI).

As on 1996-97 there were totally 263845 number of registered SSI units functioning in the state including 29445 units newly registered. The fixed capital on various assets put in operation in these units at the end of March 31st 1997 was Rs. 6395 Crore, higher by 13.62 per cent compared to 5628 Crores in 1995-96. Altogether these units employed 25.22 lakhs persons in different production functions and produced Rs. 15257 crore worth goods and services which is 13.34 per cent higher than the previous year. Tamil Nadu has accounted for 9.2 per cent of registered SSI units and 3.14 per cent of production at the national level during 1996-97.

During 1996-97 District Industries Centre (DIC) in the State has issued permanent Registration certificates to 29445

SSI units and also newly registered 7286 cottage industries and 7488 handicrafts units. The employment provided by these cottage and handicrafts units were of the order of 13073 and 13992 persons respectively.

Objectives of the Study

1. To study the performance of small scale industries in Dindigul District.
2. To study the amount of fixed capital investment in each block under various categories during the study period.
3. To study the number of person employed in each block during the study period.
4. To study the number of per cent rained under PMRY Scheme in Dindigul District.
5. To study the amount of subsidy availed by the entrepreneur in Dindigul District.

Methodology

This study is based on both primary and secondary data, primary data were collected from the entrepreneur who are registered in DIC, Secondary data have been collected from various journals, reports and periodicals for analytical purpose.

Analysis and Interpretation

Dindigul is one of the important districts in the promotion of SSI with the help and assistance of DIC. DIC is one of the important agencies engaged in the promotion of small scale units in the district and provide assistance in the form of technical support, strengthening of infrastructural facilities, supply of credit, excise duty concession, upgradation of entrepreneurial skills, necessary clearance from various departments to start new units without much delay etc.,

At the time of formation of this district on 15.09.1985 there were only 677 registered SSI units. After the establishment of DIC the growth of industries is drastically different. At the end of 31.3.97 the total no. of SSI units increased to 4779 with the investment of Rs. 1231.68 Lakh providing employment to 17629 persons. The district has got 9 types of industries such as Food based industry, Forest based industry, Animal husbandry industry, Textile based industry, Chemical based industry, Building material and cheramic industry, Engineering based industry, Electric and Electronics based industry and miscellaneous industry spread in 14 blocks in the SSI sectors. It has total fixed investment of Rs. 1462.37 Lakh in the SSI sector and provides employment.

The number of handicrafts and cottage industries registered are 3012 and 3351 respectively. To achieve this tremendous growth, DIC conducted motivation campaign, selected prospective entrepreneurs, are assisted starting from the selection of feasible schemes, providing technical guidance, financial assistance training facilities etc., upto commencement of the production in the newly started industries. In the year 1998-99 DIC has provided training to 575 persons.

The following Tables shows the performance of Small Scale Industries in Dindigul District in terms of number of industries in each block, investment in fixed assets of various industries and employment of persons in various industries in the following tables.

The number industries in each block, under the various categories during 1998-99 is tabulated in table 1.

It could be seen from the table 1 that 1055 units were started in 1998-99 in all 14 blocks in Dindigul District, which consists of 9 groups of industries. Textile industries constitute 231 units followed by Animal husbandry 166, and Engineering 155 and so on. The reason behind this was that the government gives more amounts of subsidy and concessions for starting textile industries in this district. Regarding Animal husbandry industries, they come second in this district. The cattle wealth of the District is represented by 105266 buffaloes, 36,8614 Cows, 2,83,747, Sheep 2,26,092

Table 1
Statement Showing the Blockwise Industrial Units in Various Industries in Dindigul District During 1998-1999

Sl. No.	Name of the Block	Food Based Industry	Forest based Industry	Animal husbandry Industry	Textile based Industry	Chemical based Industry	Building material and Cheramic Industry	Engineering based Industry	Electrical and Electronic based Industry	Miscellaneous Industry
1.	Dindigul	35	8	49	72	19	18	40	7	57
2.	Authoor	5	2	6	11	2	2	5	3	9
3.	Reddiyarchatram	4	2	5	12	2	3	6	2	4
4.	Sanarpatti	7	3	12	10	1	3	8	3	8
5.	Nilakkottai	10	6	10	12	2	2	11	3	9
6.	Batlagundu	12	6	9	11	2	5	12	3	20
7.	Oddanchatram	4	2	9	10	–	2	7	1	15
8.	Palani	16	4	29	43	5	9	39	5	45
9.	Thoppampatti	6	3	15	14	1	4	12	2	18
10.	Vedasandur	1	1	6	10	1	1	2	3	10
11.	Vadamadurai	5	2	7	13	2	–	6	1	9
12.	Guziliamparai	2	1	6	8	1	1	3	1	7
13.	Natham	1	1	1	2	–	1	1	–	3
14.	Kodaikanal	4	2	2	3	3	1	3	1	6
	Total	**112**	**43**	**166**	**231**	**41**	**52**	**155**	**35**	**220**

Source: Annual report DIC 1998-99.

Goats and Poultry of 5,93,024. This industry shows an encouraging trend compared to previous years figures.

The amount of fixed Capital Investment in each block under the various Categories during 1998-99 is tabulated in table 2.

Investment is an important factor for starting any type of industry including SSI. The total Fixed Investment for 9 types of industries in the year 1998-99 was Rs. 1446.17 Lakh in this District. The major fixed investment contribution goes to Textile Industry as by nature Dindigul District is suitable for textile industry after next to Coimbatore in the State. With Food and Engineering industries also have more scope. If Government considers restructing the financing of lock units in Dindigul, a large number of people will be benefited because Dindigul is famous for locks.

The number of persons employed in each block under the various categories during 1998-99 is tabulated in table 3.

Total number of workers engaged in these industries in the year 1998-1999 is around 3747 and peoples engaged in other types of industrial sectors like handicrafts, handlooms, lock and leather industry etc. are 61796. In total 65543 people are engaged in industrial activities in this district which constitute 3.72 per cent of the total population. The reason may be cited as illiteracy, lack of awareness among people about the different schemes implemented by the Government etc. Steps should be taken to include more number of people into this fold.

DIC has introduced the PMRY Scheme training for unemployment educated youth.

The following table shows the number of persons who are trained under PMRY scheme in Dindigul District.

Particulars	*93-94*	*94-95*	*95-96*	*96-97*	*97-98*	*98-99*
No. of persons (Sanctioned)	110	630	804	802	583	677
No. of persons (Trained)	80	502	679	538	696	575

Table 2

Statement Showing the Blockwise Fixed Capital Investment in Various Industries in Dindigul District During 1998-1999

Rs. Lakhs

Sl. No.	Name of the Block	Food Based Industry	Forest based Industry	Animal husbandry Industry	Textile based Industry	Chemical based Industry	Building material and Cheramic Industry	Engineering based Industry	Electrical and Electronic based Industry	Miscellaneous Industry
1.	Dindigul	21.22	7.70	126.35	132.05	69.75	14.40	29.65	1.00	70.00
2.	Authoor	1.50	1.40	0.64	6.20	2.35	1.00	1.69	0.15	6.42
3.	Reddiyarchatram	3.35	7.30	6.71	19.75	1.30	1.45	2.90	0.10	2.50
4.	Sanarpatti	4.65	2.20	1.94	15.20	2.50	5.60	3.81	0.15	9.30
5.	Nilakkottai	63.50	9.65	1.36	35.45	1.30	5.60	3.20	0.15	8.85
6.	Batlagundu	5.60	7.60	1.28	16.40	2.60	5.50	3.72	0.15	27.05
7.	Oddanchatram	2.25	2.30	1.38	18.15	–	1.70	3.26	0.05	23.25
8.	Palani	15.90	3.25	2.50	94.15	5.35	9.60	62.75	0.25	23.25
9.	Thoppampatti	53.35	7.90	1.19	65.40	0.10	7.00	6.15	0.10	13.45
10.	Vedasandur	0.45	1.00	0.62	58.10	1.75	0.60	0.30	0.15	3.20
11.	Vadamadurai	1.95	0.25	0.49	57.05	2.75	–	3.20	0.05	4.70
12.	Guziliamparai	1.10	0.30	0.59	57.45	0.05	2.00	1.40	0.05	3.10
13.	Natham	0.45	0.05	0.01	0.20	–	5.00	0.08	–	0.30
14.	Kodaikanal	1.00	0.60	0.01	0.75	0.40	0.15	0.30	0.05	9.50
	Total	**176.27**	**51.50**	**145.07**	**576.30**	**90.20**	**59.60**	**119.71**	**2.40**	**245.12**

Source: Annual report DIC 1998-99.

Table 3

Statement Showing the Blockwise Employment in Various Industries in Dindigul District During 1998-1999

Rs. Lakhs

Sl. No.	Name of the Block	Food Based Industry	Forest based Industry	Animal husbandry Industry	Textile based Industry	Chemical based Industry	Building material and Cheramic Industry	Engineering based Industry	Electrical and Electronic based Industry	Miscellaneous Industry
1.	Dindigul	139	32	125	322	86	139	126	13	52
2.	Authoor	15	9	12	35	10	23	17	5	26
3.	Reddiyarchatram	26	13	20	55	7	26	19	3	18
4.	Sanarpatti	35	14	26	41	7	15	28	5	35
5.	Nilakkottai	38	30	21	51	8	27	32	5	28
6.	Batlagundu	41	26	21	51	10	29	32	5	61
7.	Oddanchatram	20	7	24	41	—	25	20	2	3
8.	Palani	52	17	59	174	18	67	119	8	113
9.	Thoppampatti	41	20	26	87	2	34	36	3	98
10.	Vedasandur	2	4	11	53	6	20	5	5	32
11.	Vadamadurai	12	6	13	57	5	—	15	2	26
12.	Guziliamparai	6	4	9	58	3	10	10	2	24
13.	Natham	2	2	9	6	—	10	2	—	6
14.	Kodaikanal	9	8	1	8	6	2	7	2	4
	Total	**438**	**192**	**377**	**1039**	**168**	**427**	**468**	**60**	**578**

Source: Annual report DIC 1998-99.

Table 4

S. No.	Particulars	1996-1997		1997-1998		1998-1999	
		Certificate Issued	*No. of persons Employed*	*Certificate Issued*	*No. of persons Employed*	*Certificate Issued*	*No. of Persons Employed*
1.	Provisional Certificate For S.S.I.	1635	4831	1368	5301	616	2159
2.	Registered S.S.I.	977	2180	974	2211	327	441
3.	Cottage Industries	350	539	350	715	112	192
4.	Handicrafts	373	292	200	304	64	47

Table 5

List of Items	*No. of Persons Benefited*	*Amount of Subsidy and Concession Rs. in Lakhs*	*No. of Persons Benefited*	*Amount of Subsidy and Concession Rs. in Lakhs*	*No. of Persons Benefited*	*Amount of Subsidy and Concession Rs. in Lakhs*
Capital Expenditure Subsidy	35	85.92	5	5.39	6	6.15
Limited HP Subsidy	41	4.63	115	42.49	50	9.38
Generator Subsidy	4	1.22	3	0.64	6	2.23
Sales Tax/Rebate	10	211.73	3	20.30	3	102.44
Subsidy PMRY	618	289.70	536	257.24	–	–
Total	**708**	**593.20**	**662**	**326.06**	**65**	**120.20**

The table 4 shows the number of SSI Certificates issued and persons involved in respective industries.

The table 5 shows concession and subsidy availed by the entrepreneurs in Dindigul District

The table 5 reveals that the benefits obtained by the entrepreneurs were in a decreasing trend from 1996-1997 onwards. The reasons were heavy competition from large-scale sector and serious technical and economic problems.

As per the statistics given in Southern Economist May 1999, in India about 31 per cent (about 2.7. Lakhs) of the registered SSI units are either closed or sick. Due to technological absence the overall capacity utilisation in the SSI sector is merely 48 per cent in India.

Conclusion

Dindigul District is one of the important Districts for promoting more and more small-scale industries, especially in the case of agro-based areas like tomato, jasmine and mango. If government established cold storage facilities and processing center, provides technical know-how for processing, there will be changes for the establishment of more and more small-scale industries. Regarding lock units, lack of support from government authorities and lack of modern method of production cause serious threat. Leather and Textile industry face some major problems in Dindigul District, effluent treatment in leather units affect the functioning and government should come forward to encourage the small tanners by way of giving, subsidy and concession for common effluent treatment plant. It established in Dindigul and covers only the tanneries located in Southern and Western part of Dindigul alone. Recently a number of small spinning mills are closed down due to improper supply of raw materials and competition from large-scale sector. The government has to come forward to solve the perennial problems faced by the small-scale entrepreneurs in Dindigul District. It will safeguard the interest and welfare of the society at large and working community in particular.

11

Information Technology Promotes Entrepreneurship Management

*Dr. S. Maria John**

*Mrs. A. Mary Grace***

Industrial development is the backbone for economic development and industrial development envisages entrepreneurial development. Effectiveness of small enterprises depends upon the entrepreneurial and managerial capabilities of those involved in the business. Further, they require information, which should be quickly analysed and effectively implemented. Entrepreneurs create new markets and facilitate expansion into international markets. This could be achieved by the entrepreneurs with the help of Information Technology.

India is a land of enterprises and entrepreneurs, where 60% of the population is still self-employed. Self-employment has its own pros and cons. Business titans like TATA, BIRLA, DALMIA etc., have emerged successful entrepreneurs in our country, by starting business in small ways. These entrepreneurs succeeded only by adopting particular factors like skill development by experience, unpleasant action of

* Dr. S. Maria John, Reader and Research Advisor, Department of Commerce, C.P.A. College, Bodinayakanur–625 513 Tamil Nadu, (Madurai Kamaraj University).

** Mrs. A. Mary Grace, SGL in History, J.A. College, Periyakulam–625 601, (Mother Theresa University).

technology and risk bearing at all levels of business. In general a successful entrepreneur must have the qualities like technical competence, initiative, good judgment, energy, attitude, creativeness, fairness, honesty, tactfulness, emotional stability creative thinking and knowledge about Information Technology.

Entrepreneurship is meant as the function of seeking investment and production opportunity organising an enterprise to undertake a new production process, raising capital, hiring labour, arranging for supply of raw materials, finding proper location introducing new techniques on commodities, discovering new sources of raw materials and selecting top managers for day-to-day opportunities of enterprises.

It is also meant to be the ability to discover, create or invest opportunities and exploit them to the benefit of the society, which in turn brings prosperity to the innovator and his organisation.

Entrepreneurship Management

Management refers to getting things done through others. It is a multi purpose organ that manages a business, managers, workers and work. But the functional areas of management in the business enterprises that are of special interest to the entrepreneurs are marketing and sales function, accounting and finance function, production and operation function and human resources management function. Entrepreneurship Management means practices and policies not only with in the enterprises but also practices and policies outside the market. Entrepreneurship Management requires efficient management, which refers to managing all affairs of a business in a well-planned manner.

Information Technology (IT)

Information Technology can be traced way back to even as early as Rig Veda. The development of IT is one of the most significant achievements of the twentieth century. The role of IT is an instrument for progress and development has been acknowledged widely and is expected to bring in major social and economic benefits for the mankind and accelerate the process of development. IT has made greater impact on entrepreneurship. IT also refers to the paperless exchange of business information using network-based technologies.

Areas of Application of IT

IT—the fusion of computing and communications, is creating far reaching changes in the way we work, live and think. IT is a piece less resource, one of which entrepreneurs must take advantage. Small entrepreneurs who own computers with Internet technologies consider them a valuable tool, as it improves productivity and efficiently. IT plays a dominant role in the areas of applications of business to consumers, business to business and internal business process.

Business-to-Consumer

IT, between business and consumers, is accelerating the impact of information technology on consumer behaviour and business processes and markets. It establishes the interrelationships among electronic IT, consumer behaviour, and business processes and competition. So, the wide-open economic model of the Internet and the fast pace of change in Internet technologies are fundamental contributors to the development of Electronic Commerce applications between business and consumers. Retailing on the Web is an example for the same.

Business-to-Business

Business-to-Business Electronic Commerce is the wholesale side of the commercial process. For example, if a business house wants to produce and sell a product to other business houses, it must purchase raw material and a variety of contract services from other business houses in order to produce and sell a product. These activities constitute the work of business relationships. For example, Intel sells its chips to other business organisations.

Internal Business Process

The purpose behind intra organisational IT is to help a business houses to maintain relationships. This is essential to ensure superior customer service. Many business houses like software companies are customer driven and market driven. Therefore constant monitoring and evaluation of data regarding customers, suppliers, and competitors should be compiled from their web sites and discussion groups. The feed back obtained is used to shape the organisation strategies in terms of product design, advertising, customer services etc. IT facilitates managers to communicate using video conferencing, e-mail and bulletin boards so that information is better disseminated and right decisions can be made.

Today large corporate Intranets have been installed so that information can be assessed and published. Online publishing helps to reduce costs related to printing and distributing. Faster delivery of current information takes place. Since information travels faster there is a better co-ordination between the various departments. In fact all efforts are being made to convert organisations into a paperless office.

The entrepreneurs have also felt the new areas of application of IT in a large scale. The applications have brought in facilities like.

Pricing
Customer Profiles
Tele Marketing
Delivering Management
Sales Person Productivity
Profitability Reporting
Financial Forecasting
Financial Analysis
Project Management
Materials Management
Performance Evaluation
Training and Development
Government Reporting
Recruitment and Selection
Budgetary Control
Cost Analysis

Auditing
Targeted Advertisement on the web
Customer Contact and Promotion
Improving rates of Retail stores
New Product Development
Sales Analysis and Trends
Cash and Fund Flow Management
General Ledger Accounting Information
Materials Requirement Planning
Computer Aided Design (CAD)
Computer Aided Management (CAM)
Computer Integrated Manufacturing (CIM)
Man Power Planning
Personal Planning
Compensation and Incentive Planning
Labour Management Negotiations

Global Scenario of IT

In today's economic scenario, the market place is increasingly global and competitive through the growth of Internet and web based technologies. Therefore the business process requires efficient co-ordination of information between suppliers and customers with the help of e-commerce, the business will be transacted very fast. E-commerce is very useful in entrepreneurship management in the way of conducting, managing and executing business transactions and services through electronic media and networks.

Following liberalisation and global competition wealth creating is assuming paramount importance. As a result, the concept of entrepreneurship is receiving closing attention. Global entrepreneurs with innovative outlook always search for changes, respond to it and exploit as an opportunity. They are high achievers. Internet provides excellent opportunity for the existing and prospective entrepreneurs to exchange information across the world. The electronics world where we live in consists of the following viz.

EDI	-	Electronic Data Interchange
EFT	-	Electronic Fund Transfer
E-cash	-	Electronic Cash
E-stamp	-	Electronic Stamp
E-mail	-	Electronic Mail
E-Com	-	Electronic Commerce etc.,

India is known for its richness in natural resources. It provides an abundant opportunity to market our rural area products to the nook and corner of the world. The Government of India has been sanctioning huge funds for the development of IT oriented entrepreneurial development programs. The available tools of IT have also spread its wings on the individual aspects of entrepreneurship management. The various tools of IT like the Computer hardware and software including system software and application software, the electronic communications like e-mail, EDI, paging, faxing, web-publishing, the electronic conferencing including data, voice, video, teleconferencing, chat system, e-mailing system, Usenet newsgroups, the collaborative work management like knowledge management, calendaring and scheduling, the electronic information systems like expert system, office automation system decision support system, MIS, Transaction processing system and the internet technology resources including TCP/IP, client server networks, HTML, Web publishing software, web browsers, server suites, and the like have facilitated the functional areas of entrepreneurship management. With the utilisation of IT tools in an effective manner the Indian entrepreneurs are placed in an elevated plane.

12

Government Assistance Towards Rural Employment

*Dr. G. Angaiah**

*Mr. P. Rengarajan and Mr. J. Murugesan***

Introduction

In the new millenium, where population in India is crossing the one billion mark, employment generation in the un-organised sector is the only option for providing gainful employment to the millions of rural/urban youth. At present unorganised sector gives employment to about 92% of the work force in the country. Further, with the globalisation of economy, employment situation in the organised sector is not very encouraging. This further brings pressure on the un-organised sector for providing self/wage employment opportunities to a large number of rural and urban youth.

Rural development and poverty alleviation in India has always been one of the main objectives of planning since its inception. But till the third five year plan, the emphasis was on the growth in gross national product and it was assumed that it would trickle down to masses and enhance their income levels. But it did not happen as assumed. The Green

* Dr. G. Angaiah M. Com., M. Phil., Ph. D. Research Advisor, Head, Department of Commerce, Government Arts College, Udumalpet.

** Mr. P. Rengarajan and Mr. J. Murugesan M.Com., M. Phil., Research Scholar in Commerce, Vidyasagar College of Arts and Science, Udumalpet.

Revolution had also by passed both the poor and the backward areas. Even today about 27% of the rural population is subsisting below the poverty.

Role of Government

Generation of self-employment for the poor in rural areas is one of the important components of anti-poverty and rural development strategy adopted by the Ministry of Rural Development, Government of India, Swarnajayanthi Gram Swarozgar Yojana (hereafter referred to as SGSY) is the major on going programme for self employment generations for the marginalised sections of rural communities. This programme came into being on 1st April, 1999 after merging the Integrated Rural Development Programme (IRDP), Training of Rural Youth for Self-employment (TRYSEM), Development of Women and Children in Rural Areas (DWCRA), Supply of Improved Toolkits to Rural Artisans (SITRA), Ganga Kalyan Yojana (GKY) and Million Well Scheme (MWS). SGSY is a centrally sponsored scheme, which is being funded by the centre and the states in the ratio of 75:25.

Why this Yojana?

Prof. S.R. Hashim Committee recommended for a single self-employment programme, suggested for making efforts towards from individual beneficiaries approach to group approach in implementation of self generation programme and preference to group activities and cluster approach. It was admitted that the multiplicity of programmes being viewed as separate programme in themselves resulted in a lack of proper social intermediation, absence of desired linkages among these programmes, inter-se and the implementation being concerned with achieving individual, programme targets rather than focussing on the substantive issues of sustainable income generation.

To overcome these bottlenecks in the process of generation of employment opportunities, this, holistic programme, encompassing all aspects of self-employment such as organisation of the poor into self-help groups, training, credit, technology, infrastructures and marketing was evolved.

As this scheme, particularly focuses on the vulnerable groups, special safe guards have been provided to them by way of earmarking 50%, benefits for SCs/STs, 40% for women and 10% for the disable persons.

SGSY is aimed at bringing the assisted poor families (Swarozgaries, above the poverty line in three years by providing them income-generating assets through a way of bank credit and government subsidy, ensuring atleast Rs. 2,000 net income to the assisted families.

Strategy

Three approaches have been adopted to tackle the problem of poverty of beneficiaries through creating self employment in rural areas in under SGSY.

Individual Swarozgaries

Individual swarozgaries are selected in the meeting of gram sabha as well as by a team of 3 members consisting of Block Development Officer or his representative, the banker and Sarpanch (Gram Panchayat President) with the involvement and guidance of the District Rural Development agency.

Group of Swarozgaries

This programme focuses in organisation of the poor in the form of self-help group (consisting of 10-20 persons). However in case of minor irrigation and in case of disabled persons this number may be a minimum of 5 through the process of social mobilisation (SM) for their poverty eradication.

Special Projects

The projects may involve different strategies to provide long term sustainable self-employment opportunities either in terms of organisation of the rural poor, provision of support for infrastructure, technology, marketing, training etc. Fifteen per cent of the funds under SGSY are set aside for special projects

Activity Clusters

For this 4-5 key activities are to be identified for each block based in the resources, occupational skill of the people and availability of markets. These key activities are preferably be taken up in clusters order to establish effective backward and forward linkages for harvesting economies of large scale production.

Infrastructure Development

Adequate infrastructure is essential for the success of micro-enterprises for production processing, quality testing, storage or marketing. In order to fill the critical gaps in investment 20% of the total allocation made under SGSY is earmarked for this activity in each district.

Technology and Market Support

SGSY attempts to ensure upgradation of technology in 4-5 identified key activities. The technology intervention seeks to value addition, linkages with agriculture and animal husbandry extension services and productive enhancement, efficient improvement, cost effectiveness etc.,

For sustained production of goods and services, suitable market is essential. One of the drawbacks in the earlier version of self employment programme was their concentration on the inputs rather than output (finished products) and their marketing. To rectify this situation, SGSY provides assures for promotion of marketing of the goods produced by the swarozgaries by way of involvement and participation of them in exhibition melas at international, national, state and sub-state levels. Besides, provision of market intelligence, development of market and consultancy as well as institutional arrangements for marketing of goods, including exports are made.

Financial Assistance

SGSY is a credit-cum-subsidiary programme. Credit here is a critical component in the scheme. Subsidy being only a minor and enabling element. Subsidy under SGSY is uniform at 30% of the project cost, subject to a maximum of Rs. 7,500/-. However for SC/STs subsidy is 50% and Rs. 10,000/- respectively. For groups of swarozgaries (i.e. self help groups) the subsidy is at 50% of the cost of the scheme, subject to a ceiling of Rs. 1.25 Lakh. All SGSY loans are treated as medium term loans with minimum repayment period of 5 years.

Implementation

SGSY is being implemented by DRDA (District Rural Development Agency) through the intermediate tier of the Panchayati Raj system and with the active involvement of Panchayati Raj institutions, the banks, the line departments, and the non-governmental organisation. In order to ensure proper and effective co-ordination, committees at block, district, state, and control levels have been constituted under the scheme.

(ii) Self Help Groups: [SHG]

This concept has been launched to provide self employment and economic empowerment to the rural poor on the initiation of the Ministry of Rural Development. It has been decided in a national inference in June, 2001 to raise the members of self help groups in the country, from the existing 5.11 lakhs to 10 lakhs by the year 2004, so as to have atleast one viable self help group in each rural habitation in the country.

As a set up of awareness and non-formal is integral to the activities of any voluntary agency, such SGHs not only provide the members with an opportunity to carry out economic activities, but also discuss and analyse their social and economic situations to arrive at the root cause of their problems and strive to find and implement solutions. Self Help Groups, therefore, become a forum for the collective voice of the poor against common oppression and exploitation to understand individual and common problems and improving their skills and capacities to manage resources.

Objectives of SHG

- Improves discipline on group members in developing saving habit

- Savings enhance self confidence of the individual as it is a sign of group encouragement.
- Group savings of the poor can demonstrate the strength of unity of members.
- Savings can cover the individual's risk against normal business risk.

Self Help Groups may take up the following economic activities:

- They may take up individual activities like farming, animal husbandry, artisan work, petty trade and wage labour.
- They may also come together to our common investments like a common well, agro-service center.
- They may also take up joint activities like social forestry with joint responsibility and involvement to generate employment to earn livelihood.

Functions

SHG's are mostly informal groups where members pool savings as a thrift deposit. The groups have common perception of need and improve towards collective activity may such groups formed around specific production activities, promote savings among members and use the pooled resources to meet the various credit needs of members.

Where funds generation is low in the initial phases due to low saving capacities. This is supplemented by external resources. Thus self help groups have been able to provide primitive banking service to its members that are cost effective, flexible and without defaults, based on local requirements.

Training for Enterprising Women

Under DWCRA scheme training an opportunity to learn from their own family members. Women groups are producing of more than 50 varieties of productions. The important items manufactured by them are hosiery, brass items, candles, cane items, carpets, chappals, chilli powder, coir items, doll making, dairy farm, agar bathi items, vermiculture, food masala powders, khadi and leather goods, papads pickles, plastic items, wooden furniture etc.

Socio-Economic Status

This survey was conducted by DRDA, reveals that DWCRA Bazaar helped rural women to earn an additional monthly income ranging from Rs. 500 to Rs. 2500 depending on the enterprising activities taken up by them. The survey also revealed that nearby 48% of women groups involved in the production are in the age group of 19-35 years and more than 60% of the members are in the age group of 19-50 years.

(iii) Community Polytechnics

This scheme was instituted under Direct Central Assistance in 1978-79 in 36 selected polytechnics on an experimental basis. The scheme, envisaged the community polytechnics to act as total points for science and technology applications in rural areas and to generate self and wage employment opportunities through non-formal training.

The community polytechnics carry out the following activities.

- Socio-Economic Technological Survey
- Man Power Development and Training
- Transfer of Technology
- Technical Support Services
- Community
- Dissemination of Information

Based on the demand from various state governments, the scheme was expanded gradually and it is now covering 739 polytechnics in the country. It is expected that all AICTE recognised polytechnics will be covered during the tenth five year plan period. It has contributed directly and indirectly in employment opportunities in rural areas.

Employment Generation

- Depending upon the requirement, multi skill training is also provided in various vocation trades.
- Each community polytechnic trains about 400-500 rural youth in a year.
- About 10-15% of the total trainees are setting up self employment.
- About 20-25% are wage employed. They are also getting personal jobs in various state/Central Government employment schemes.
- About 5-10% of the rural youth, even after taking training are working as agricultural labourers.

Employment Generated through Various Schemes

(i) Direct Wage Employment

Under this scheme some of the pass-outs from the community polytechnic get employment as instructors/ supervisors.

(ii) Wage Employment in Rural Industries/Service Sector

Wage employment opportunities in rural areas are also available in rural industries and in the service sector.

For Example: Persons trained in fabrication, welding, plumbing, and other civil engineering trades etc., get self employment in rural areas.

(iii) Wage-Employment

Under this category of programme wage-employment is given to the poor on various public works. The Sampoorna Grameen Rozgar Yojana (SGRY) was launched on 25th Sep. 2001 with the purpose to take care of food security, additional wage employment and creating village infrastructure in rural areas after merging erstwhile Jawahar Gram Samiridhi Yojana (JGSY) and Employment Assurance Yojana (EAS). It may be mentioned that JGSY was earlier known as Jawahar Rozgar Yojana (JRY) came into being in 1989 after merging erstwhile National Rural Employment Programme (NREP) and Rural Employment Guarantee Programme (RLEGP)/MPs local development scheme also comes under this category of the programme.

(iv) Special Areas Development Programme

Programmes under this head are aimed at creation of infrastructure in the backward areas which also give employment to marginalised sections of rural areas. Drought Prone Areas Programme (DPAP), Desert Development Programme (DDP) and Integrated Waste Land Development Programme (IWDP) come under this approach of poverty alleviation and rural development.

(v) New Scheme

Jai Prakash Rozgar Guarantee Yojana (JPRGY) to be launched to provide employment guarantee to the unemployed in the most distressed Districts of the country. This task force headed by the Minister for Rural Development, KVIC, Development Commissioner, SSI and other agencies would be fully involved in the implementation of this scheme.

Conclusion

With introduction of economic reforms, potential of employment available in unorganised sector should be kept in mind. To enhance the productivity of unorganised sector there is a great need for well trained and competent youth in various vocations. So the above said schemes had taken a good initiative and will prove a mile stone in this direction

13

Commercial Banks and Entrepreneurship Development

*Prof. R. Ramesh**
*Prof. S. Suresh***

Entrepreneurship is a complex phenomenon viewed differently by different people. Some think of entrepreneur primarily as "innovators" with dynamism in their approach. Entrepreneurial potential can be found and developed ir-respective of socio-economic backgrounds, location, sex, age, qualifications or experiences. It is, therefore, necessary to generate and transmit this feeling among the unemployed youth to sow the seed of Entrepreneurship. Instead of aspiring for white collared jobs, the educated unemployed youth are to be motivated to become efficient and successful entrepreneurs.

Entrepreneurship in India

The performance of the post independence economy is well documented until independence, on the part of our countrymen were discouraged by all possible means. The Indian economy was literally stagnant in the pre-independence period.

* Prof. R. Ramesh M.B.A., Lecturer, Department of Management Studies, A.V.V.M Sri Pushpam College (Autonomous), Poondi, Thanjavur. (Tamil Nadu).

** Prof. S. Suresh M. Com., M. Phil., Lecturer, Department of Commerce, A.V.V.M Sri Pushpam College (Autonomous) Poondi, Thanjavur. (Tamil Nadu).

To set this anomaly right, after independence, Indian planners launched a series of Five year Plans aimed at pooling our scarce resources together and through that build up infrastructure such as major core industries, irrigation and power projects, etc. However in its over enthusiasm to ration and optimise the scarce resources, the government put in place a maze of regulations which somewhere down the line lost sight of its original purpose. This resulted in an economy shackled by over administration and over regulation effectively stifling any entrepreneurial initiative. As a result of this protectionism, Indian industry grew increasingly lethargic and obsolute.

This naturally affected the Indian performance in the external sector where our products were no match to the technically and qualitatively superior foreign goods and services.

In a developing country like India, the role of entrepreneurs supporting and backing up the government efforts to accelerate the harnessing of the vast resources. The infrastructure that was built during the process has given rise to derementous opportunities to the enterprising people to set up various ventures putting to use various resources including men and material. The contribution of these private enterprise is quite significant both in terms of employment and National income.

Role of Commercial Banks

The main functional area through which commercial banks can help in developing entrepreneurship is the development of credit. The timely availability of adequate credit at reasonable rates of interest with flexible repayment conditions can go a long way in entrepreneurship development by attenuating uncertainty and facilitating risk while making available the capital needed by the people for undertaking self employment activities. Through consultancy and merchant banking functions the banks are further making earnest efforts in entrepreneurship development by (a) helping the identification of viable schemes and formulation of bankable projects for self employment (b) importing training and (c) ensuring advisory services.

The major area in which commercial banks contributes for enterpreneurship development are ancillary, tiny and small industries, agro based village/cottage industries, business and trade. Public sector commercial bank have formulated and implemented various schemes to promote the development of entrepreneurship. Bank role in promoting self employment opportunities to the educated unemployed youth through schemes such as CMEY, PMRY etc. are noteworthy.

SBI, one of the biggest commercial banks in India, to promote entrepreneurship sanctioned Rs. 12,718 crore to small scale industries. The project finance strategic business unit of SBI focuses on core and infrastructure sector, like power, telecommunications, oil and gas, roads, bridges, ports and urban infrastructure. By the end of March 2002, the Bank total sanctions to infrastructure sector stood at Rs. 18,556 crore comprising 112 projects. Projectuptech, set up by SBI in 1998 for bringing about technology upgradation of small and medium enterprises, has taken up 15 projects to so far in India. Corporate Accounts Group of SBI, which provides a wide range of financial services through Relationship Banking to the top entrepreneurs in India advanced Rs. 16,943 crore as at the end of March 2002. SBI corporate loan scheme, launched during 1999-2000, was well received by the entrepreneur clients and over Rs. 1400 crore of such loans were sanctioned 60 various entrepreneurs during the year 2000-2001.

Banking are facing problems in identification of right type of people with potential entrepreneurial skill. The problem of identification is found to be more serious in case of small enterprises. Further, inadequate infrastructure, non-conductive environment particularly in rural areas, less or non availability of basic inputs mounting overdues are also some of the bottlenecks in the entrepreneurial development efforts by commercial banks. To overcome me above problems in the field of entrepreneurship development. It is essential to continuously recise and envolve various support systems to specifically address the various inhibiting factors. This process involves selection of entrepreneurs, their training, consultation during pre-investment and post investment stages and financing etc.

Conclusion

India is one of the very few countries in the world, which has developed a wide range of agencies (STDVI, IFCI, ICICI, IDBI etc.,) aimed at developing entrepreneurship. These agencies have certainly filled a vital gap in the industrial development programme of India by meeting the widespread and varying needs of entrepreneurial activity. They have been a valuable source of information to the prospective entrepreneurs about the various opportunities available. In addition to this, they have been providing entrepreneurial development in the country. Besides these agencies commercial Banks are the main financial institutions which look into the financing of Project.

14

Role of Income Tax on Entrepreneurship Management

*S. Suresh**

Introduction

In most developing countries, the taxation policy aims at the promotion of agriculture and Industry. Industrial development may, however, be stimulated by means of a reduction in the normally applicable tax liability in the form of either an exemption from income-tax on the amount invested (or) a concession in the tax rate or a reduction in tax profit.

In the early stages of the developmental programmes for small-scale-industries, the Government had provided a number of taxation benefits with adequate incentives. In fact, special tax concessions to small-scale industries are desirable for the accumulation of capital and for directing it into right channels.

Taxation Benefits to Small-Scale Industries

The taxation benefits available to SSI, are enumerated below:

I. Tax Holiday

New industrial undertakings, including SSI, exempted

* S. Suresh M. Com., M. Phil., Lecturer, Dept of Commerce, A.V.V.M Sri Pushpam College (Autonomous), Poondi, Thanjavur. (Tamil Nadu).

from the payment of income tax under section 80J of the Act on their profits up to 6 per cent p.a of the capital employed. The deduction at the rate of 6 per cent from the total income is allowed in the assessment year in which the unit begins to manufacture, provided that the conditions specified in section 80J are fulfilled by SSI. This concession is for five years from the commencement of production.

Small-scale units should satisfy the following conditions before they become eligible for tax benefits:

1. They should not have been formed by the splitting or reconstitution of an existing unit;
2. They should employ 10 (or) more workers in a manufacturing process with power (or) 20 or more persons without power.

II. Depreciation

Under section 32 of the Income Tax Act, a small-scale industry is entitled to deduction on depreciation account on Buildings, Furniture, Plant and Machinery at the prescribed rates.

In the case of SSI, the deduction from the actual cost of plant and machinery is allowed up to Rs. 20 lakhs; in the case of any machinery or plant hired by a unit, the actual cost there of the owner of such machinery or plant.

III. Deduction when Disallowed

The deduction of depreciation allowance will not be allowed in respect of:

(i) Any machinery or plant installed in any office premises to any residential accommodation, including any accommodation in the nature of a guest house;

(ii) Any machinery or plant in respect of which the deduction by way of development rebate is allowable under section 33; and

(iii) Any machinery (or) plant installed after 31st March 1976.

IV. *Rehabilitation Allowance*

Under section 33B, a rehabilitation allowance is granted to any small-scale industries undertaken in India, whose business is discontinued on account of:

(i) Flood, typhoon, huricane, cyclone, earth-quake, or other natural upheaval;

(ii) Riot or civil disturbance;

(iii) Accidental Fire (or) explosion;

(iv) Action by an enemy

The rehabilitation allowance is used for business purpose with in three years. After reconstruction the unit can deduct a sum equivalent to 60 per cent of the amount of the deduction allowable to the unit.

V. *Investment Allowance*

One of the most useful tax concession offered to small scale units under the Income Tax Act is the deduction by way of investment allowance granted under section 3A. It was introduced in 1976, replacing the initial depreciation allowance. The investment allowance is granted at the rate of 25 per cent the cost of acquisition of new plant (or) machinery installed, unlike the development rebate, which was allowed at different rates ranging from 10 per cent to 40 per cent.

The unit which wants to avail this benefit, should utilise the machinery (or) plant either in the year of installation (or) in the immediate following year, otherwise, the unit cannot avail the benefits.

VI. *Other Concessions*

SSI undertakings are also entitled to claim the various tax benefit granted to other tax-payers such as,

1. Rehabilitation allowance
2. Expenditure on specific development allowance
3. Rural development allowance
4. Agricultural development allowance

5. Allowance of expenses by way of contribution for rural development, and
6. Other deductions allowed in computing the taxable income from business.
7. Relaxations to small-scale industries regarding excise duty.

Conclusion

Tax concession have two important objectives, namely,

1. To promote investment in SSI and
2. To provide relief to them.

Tax concession are used to stimulate the establishment (or) expansion of SSI in a desirable manner. In addition, tax concessions are also provided for new investments in particular industries or specific localities.

The future of the SSI by and large depends upon the industrial policy pursued by the Government during the nineties. The small-scale sector requires, the active support of the Government it is, therefore, necessary to adopt a policy conducive to the growth of this sector, so as to enable it to enter the 21st century with confidence and bright prospects.

References

1. P. Saravanavel, *Entrepreneurial Development.*
2. Dr. Vasant Desai, *Small Scale Industries and Entrepreneurial.*
3. Dr. V. Balan, *Entrepreneurial Development.*

15

Conceptual Framework for the Pattern of Cooperative Entrepreneurship

*M. Karthikeyan and R. Karunakaran**

Economic development originates and fosters in relation to the strength and health of the local entrepreneurship and depends on the rate of its generation and equally to the intensity of its sense of social responsibility, its innovation quotient and its index of management capabilities. Entrepreneurial density, innovative propensity and management capability in the society in a particular period determine the character and future of economic development.

Entrepreneurs are rarely mentioned in connection with cooperative development, which reflects the state of entrepreneurship in conventional economic thinking, where entrepreneurs are more often than not a missing category.

Need for Cooperative Entrepreneurship

In cooperative theory and policy, is not aware of any approach which has addressed the connection between entrepreneurial behaviour and the degree of economic success and failure of cooperatives. Policy makers have theoritised, planned and implemented in a virtual vacuum about

* M. Karthikeyan and R. Karunakaran, Research Scholar and Lecturer, Department of Cooperation, Gandhigram Rural Institute, Gandhigram, Tamil Nadu.

cooperative entrepreneurship is causally related to the main effects of economic growth (increase in incomes, productivity, employment, living standards), not to include entrepreneurial activity in cooperative policy bias and even policy errors. Preventing the potential of cooperatives for development from being used sufficiently and effectively, when innovative entrepreneurship is a necessary condition for the achievement of economic development in general and an organisation's success in specific, there can be no question that cooperative entrepreneurs will have to be included; withcut cooperative entrepreneurship, cooperatives cannot succeed, they will not even be established.

Cooperative entrepreneurship refers to a role or a set of roles whose influences are conditioned by characteristics of group members. The personalities of the entrepreneurs are influenced by the situation. But the true entrpreneurship though individual oriented has got a collective group foundation in cooperatives. Cooperative entrepreneurs collectively engage in the enterprise activity for the economic interest of themselves.

Cooperative entrepreneurship should function collectively and should have courage to stand up when something wrong is done and should be capable of owning a mistake openly. Such cooperative entrepreneurs will not only succeed but will also make the cooperatives a succeed story in the world.

Cooperative Entrepreneur-Definition

"Cooperative Entrepreneur is one who undertakes and assumes the responsibility to discovery innovate cooperative opportunity, on the basis of collective effort, which has the cooperative effect for the socio-economic development of the member entrepreneurs simultaneously with the cooperative values". The Author.

Principles of Cooperative Entrepreneurship

1. Principle of innovation
2. Principle of cooperation
3. Principle of active participation

4. Principle of democratic management
5. Principle of communication and information
6. Principle of collective decision making
7. Principle of honesty and opens (self confidence)
8. Principle of cooperative development thro' entrepreneurial development
9. Principle of social responsibility
10. Principle of time management

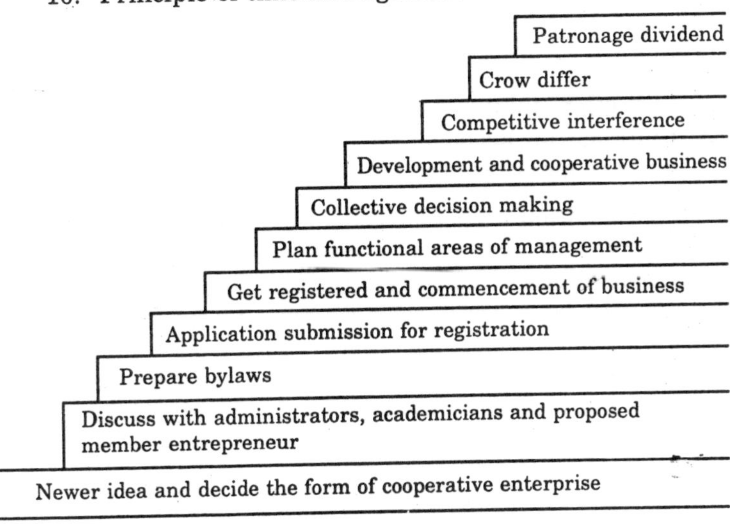

Pattern of Cooperative Entrepreneurship

1. Cooperative entrepreneurs are part of the class of members (member entrepreneur)
2. Cooperative entrepreneurs are managers of the cooperative enterprise (Executive entrepreneur).
3. Director entrepreneurs are elected from among the members as representatives to administer the cooperative enterprise. (Director Entrepreneur).
4. Cooperative entrepreneurs are part of a governmental or parastatal administration

bureaucratic entrepreneurs (bureaucratic entrepreneur)

5. Cooperative entrepreneurs are members of other non-cooperative organisation (such as schools, universities, donor/aid and sponsoring agencies, churches) who provide career possibilities and incentives independent from or in addition to cooperative entrepreneurship (catalytic entrepreneur).

From these five patterns of cooperative entrepreneurship, the first three can be characterised as effort taking, the other two as external, promoting entrepreneurs.

In effort taking cooperative entrepreneurship, the vital entrepreneurial decisions are made by person with function within a cooperative society.

In addition cooperatives can be established through the initiative of external agents: functionaries from administrations which very often have been set up especially to organise and assist cooperatives are responsible for the establishment of cooperative organisation: bureaucratic entrepreneur. Usually, but not necessarily, this type of entrepreneurship implies the "officialisation" of the cooperative movement.

But cooperative can be promoted by outsiders in another way: person who specialise in local institutional development are endowed with responsibilities for getting mutual self help processes stared. These catalysts can be paid professionals of volunteers, employed by the government or non-government organisation.

Member as Entrepreneur

In some sense, if a cooperative entrepreneur is also a member of the cooperative, even in a cooperative some element of private commercial activity may be retained.

Quite often we can observe cooperatives directed by a "big man" or a small group of important figure which seem to run the cooperative like an extended family business.

In this way, they are appropriating, quite legally and endorsed by the by-laws of the cooperative society, and often with the consent of the members, a substantial share of the benefits and wealth created by the cooperative.

This kind of entrepreneurial pattern normally assumes, in order to be successful, a high level of member-heterogeneity, and may result in a quite unequal distribution of the wealth created.

But again, these outcomes of members entrepreneurship should not surprise us, given the difficulties and peculiarities of cooperatives action, the unequal appropriation of cooperative wealth is one of the few realistic avenues open for spontaneous cooperative entrepreneurship and hence for spontaneous cooperative evolution.

In addition, the dominance of one or few entrepreneurial decision-makers in a cooperative may tend to reduce the transaction costs of collective decision making in cooperatives, very often on reason of competitive disadvantages of cooperatives.

The member entrepreneur in cooperation corresponds to the intrapreneurs is a public corporation (public limited company) who own equity (or options for the acquisition of equity) as holders of corporate equity or shares they are (as other—non managerial/entrepreneurial owners/shareholders) residual claimants of the variability in the operation of the firm.

Executives as Entrepreneurs

We observed that those individuals creating and implementing cooperative opportunities will not necessarily be identical with those who manage the ongoing cooperative. This will be the case especially during the initiating or founding phase of a cooperative venture.

Some of the externality or public good difficulties resulting from the non-existing or weak rights of entrepreneurs to appropriate contractual and residual wealth create by his actions can be overcome if the entrepreneur becomes a cooperative manager.

Executive (manager) require, to successfully adapt the cooperative to a changing environment and changing needs of the members, the right of autonomous decision opportunities for managerial opportunism. A 'high' level of participation allows the members to constrain opportunities, but not to eliminate it, given asymmetrical information or positive transaction costs. Consequently, there is no way that members can completely prevent the appropriation of benefits belonging to them as the owner users.

It is naïve to assume that members are able, under realistic assumptions, to monitor diligently, effectively and efficiently the performance of the manager and the cooperative entrepreneur and operate a powerful system of checks and balances on management.

Managers do not necessarily share the objectives of the members owners. They have some choice in the direction, pace, quality, and duration of their efforts, depending, among other factors on the effectiveness of members participation and the cooperative's external environment. Managerial discretion has to be recognised as a fact commercial life also in cooperatives.

Directors as Entrepreneurs

The board members are elected as representatives from among the members democratically following the principles of 'one member one vote'. The board members are responsible for the administration of a cooperative where they have the board membership. They are the internal administrative entrepreneurs to look after the affairs of the cooperative enterprise.

Board members elect the president and vice-president in order to delegate authority and responsible. The president is the head of a cooperative enterprise in all respects.

Bureaucrats as Entrepreneurs

One prominent and very often also empirically attempted solution to the problems of incentive failure in cooperative has been the take over of entrepreneurial functions by the government: government officials in open of disgusted form, try to act as cooperative entrepreneur.

This remedy to incentive failure is theoretically equivalent to the government provision of 'public goods'. In many developing countries, it seems a standard solution to the problems and failures of spontaneous evolution of cooperatives.

With this approach, plans, polices and strategies are fixed at the top, then carried out through a hierarchical system of rules, regulations and commands.

The entrepreneurial contribution consists in identifying and determining the correct courses of action others have to follow and in implementing the "project".

The blue print, up-down or synoptic approach may indeed succeed in establishing cooperatives: by bureaucratic command or force, officials are required to set up cooperative societies. Following the colonial model, the government works at the local level, and often through local leaders.

Usually, the government uses the cooperative to channel inputs to or obtain produce from the members, in order to achieve government objectives and maintain or obtain political support, and cooperative are or become officialised of the government.

Even if the government provision of cooperative entrepreneurs can be considered as a solution to the incentive difficulties, in reality it has been more often than not an inadequate, dysfunctional and harmful solution.

Hierarchical control, or supervision, become indispensable and hierarchical incentives (power, prestige, rank and status) the main motivators for entrepreneurial action.

Catalytic Entrepreneurs

The first two must cater to members demands, even if these demands may be satisfied inequality. In an idealistic (nirwana) cooperative, all members are equal. In real life cooperative ventures, some members are more equal than others. Otherwise, it would be difficult to get cooperatives off the ground: internalisation of the external benefits created by entrepreneurial action increases entrepreneurial rewires; the entrepreneurs can use the property rights of members or a manager to appropriate for himself more of the benefits created by his action.

To 'solve' the incentive problems in cooperatives, we can substitute bureaucratic entrepreneurs for private cooperative entrepreneurs, but only at the cost of lower efficiency, effectiveness and member involvement and very probably, and—historically usually the case—by giving up the philosophy and motivation of cooperative self-help. Self-help motivation, a characteristic of the first two patterns, will be washed out by the flood of resources, regulations and commands that the government pours into the cooperatives.

A fourth pattern of cooperative entrepreneurship may offer some hope to circumvent (evade) the problems of the entrepreneurial approached discussed so far, since it provides entrepreneurial incentives and can work from bottom up.

Catalytic entrepreneurs are external agents, or members of outside agencies, whose task it is to get the process of cooperative institutionalisation started and to work with and strengthen local cooperatives these outside cooperative entrepreneurs (or agencies) can be governmental or non-governmental. What makes the "catalyst" different from the bureaucratic entrepreneur is that

1. he is not working through conventional bureaucratic or technological channels and
2. the local cooperative institutions he is initiating, promoting and supporting remain autonomous. Self-organising organisations, i.e., do not become an officialised and regulated part of a governmental or parastatal administration.

Catalytic entrepreneurs, then, are specialists in the initialisation, promotion and support of cooperative organisations.

The designations for such persons are various. The terms "promoter", "change agent", "facilitator", "motivator" have been used. The term "catalyst" is, as Uphoff (1986, p. 207) argues, "probably more neutral and more descriptive implying that the person initiates a change process but is not absorbed by it".

External, assistance, promotion and entrepreneuring may be in contradiction to the philosophy of cooperative self-help.

Since part of the benefits are external to the promotor or cooperative projector, it is only logical, and from an economic point of view rational and consistent to compensate for this divergence by external assistance, without external promotion, not very much will happen with cooperative self-help. To think otherwise is naïve and idyllic.

The limits to self-initiating cooperatives will be the more server, the poorer and the more homogenous the members are: homogeneity tends to eliminate the incentives for the spontaneous foundation of cooperatives by members-entrepreneurs.

Unfortunately, cooperatives established and managed by government administrators also have a tendency to crow out poor members: the poor have nothing to provide to the achievement national target, and the poor lose out in the struggle for access to the handouts by the cooperatives.

16

The Perspective of Co-Operative Entrepreneurship—Need of the Hour

Dr. Samwel Kakuko Lopoyetum

Introduction: An overview

Industrialisation and Agricultural development can be achieved both by collective means and individual means through innovative initiatives. These are all forms of entrepreneurship. Usually the individuals and groups as Entrepreneurs are the most important persons in economic life and natural resources gain value by their ingenuity, if there is failure, they forge success through "failure knowledge" to ensure "social and economic stability in the long-run". Entrepreneurship is neither science nor an art, it is actually a practice. An entrepreneur is essentially a creative person or an innovative person. He must be interested to acquaint himself with advancing technology and improving the quality of his services and products. He must also expand and reinvest in the organisation or enterprise or firm. The importance of entrepreneurship in socio-economic development through cooperative sector need not be over emphasised. It is useful in promotion of industrial growth and business

* Dr. Samwel Kakuko Lopoyetum, Senior Post-Doctoral Research Fellow (PDRF) Department of Co-operation, Gandhigram Rural Institute (Nationally Accredited with Five Star Status by NAAC), Gandhigram-624 302, Tamil Nadu.

ventures and also for the socio-economic prosperity of the community.

Inadequate availability of entrepreneurial talent adversely affected the development of modern manufacturing processing and marketing enterprises. Entrepreneurship is a function which seeks investment and production process by raising capital, arranging labour, and raw materials, finding site, introducing new techniques and commodities and discovering new sources for the enterprise.

Definition of Co-operative Entrepreneurship

"Co-operative entrepreneurship deals with undertaking and assuming the responsibility to discover/innovate/initiate co-operative opportunity on the basis of the collective efforts which has co-operative effects for higher growth of cooperative organisations and better socio-economic pattern of entrepreneurs members and community by simultaneously applying co-operative values, co-operative principles accompanied by the management principles/practices"— Dr. Samwel Kakuko Lopoyetum (GRI 2003) and Mr. M. Karthikeyan (GRI 2003).

The New Perspective of Co-operative Entrepreneurship

The Indian economic policy since 1991, had paradigmatically shifted and paved way for new implications such as competitiveness, transparency, marketisation and operational efficiency, productivity parameters have brought unimaginable shifts and switches in the economic environment. Co-operative sector is basically democratic sector, but co-operative should be naturally be guided and led by informed and entrepreneurial leaders. Leadership in co-operative is to ensure that, the organisation is developed and ventures become successful and also carry on the business in accordance with the co-operative principles. The application of management principles and practices in co-operative entrepreneurship is highly desirable in this regard. The principle of voluntary and open membership, democratic member control remains vital in running enterprises. There is an urgent need to change the attitudes and business activities of the co-operative enterprises. Co-operatives perform two functions simultaneously, *viz.,* services to members and achieve business goals. Survival of the co-operative enterprise is highly essential in the era of open market economy. Even though, a number of successful stories of co-operative like 'Amul' and 'Warna Model' remain the pillar stone in the co-operative sector, still we need and require co-operative entrepreneurship leadership in co-operative sector. It is surely the need of the hour, Co-operatives have the ability to transform the socio-economic condition of crores of underprivileged population in India and Kenya, therefore, co-operative entrepreneurship leadership is required. Co-operative enterprises are formed to meet the needs of the members. The success of any co-operative primarily depends on the members participation in its business and management, therefore the entrepreneurial culture among the members are essential. The principle of self-help and voluntarism of co-operative are necessary and consistent with the entrepreneurial framework of the co-operative organisations. The new National Policy on co-operatives should recognise the need for inculcating the spirit of entrepreneurship culture in the co-operative sector. The guiding principle in formulating the National Policy on cooperatives must emanate from the elements and parameters of entrepreneurship.

Quantitative Growth and Progress: One of the most notable factor in the cooperative sector (see table 1) is overwhelming quantitative growth of cooperative sector and percentage of share in the national economy. It can be termed as extremely massive in quantitative terms but qualitatively low. The coverage is simply excellent. It covers larger part of the Indian Economy, hence the need of the hour is inculcating the culture of cooperative entrepreneurship.

Developing Entrepreneurial Competencies in Co-operative Sector

In the advent of LPG's, it is essential for the co-operative sector to understand what types of inbuilt competencies are available with them. They need to apply SWOT/SCOT analysis with reference to entrepreneurship development. It is highly

Table 1
Growth and progress of cooperative sector in India

S. No.	*Details*	*% share in the national economy*
1.	Rural network (Villages covered)	100%
2.	Agricultural credit disbursed (NABARD)	46.3
3.	Fretiliser disbursed (5.809 million tones)	31.0
4.	Sugar produced (7.062 Million tones)	54.9
5.	Capacity utilisation of sugar mills	90.1
6.	Wheat procurement	29.7
7.	Jute procurement (1995-96)	21.0
8.	Retail fair price shops (1,25,200)	28.5
9.	Milk procurement to total production	6.7
10.	Milk procurement to marketable surplus	10.0
11.	Oil Marketed (branded)	51.0
12.	Spindles in cooperative (3.27 million)	10.5
13.	Cotton market/procurement (1997)	72.9
14.	Cotton yarn/fabrics production	19.3
15.	Cotton yarn export	8.0
16.	Handlooms in cooperatives	55.0
17.	Fisherman is cooperative (active)	21.5
18.	Storage facility (village levels PACs)	62.0
19.	Soyabean production	7.5
20.	Self employment generated for persons in (in millions)	12.5
21.	Salt manufactured	7.5

Source: NCUI, 1999, Indian Cooperative Movement, A Profile, p. 6.

desirable and essential to promote entrepreneurship culture in all cooperative sub sectors which would result in qualitative improvement of cooperative sector at large. It is the highest time that the co-operative sector should introspect and evaluate itself and strengthen its modern competencies. They need to evolve new pattern of behaviour in the era LPG and open market economy such as (1) Concern for high quality of products, services and manufacturing processes. (2) Use of Information Technology and advanced communication technology. (3) Adopt the culture of efficiency and effectiveness in their operations. (4) Self confidence and leadership. (5) Use of modern management strategies. (6) Professionalisation of management process and modernisation of machines. (7) Quality upgradation. (8) Financial support measures. (9) Promotion of new enterprises. (10) Provision of in-puts and technical assistance/knowledge. (11) Minimisation of risks (12) Reduction of cost of production.

Need for Promoting Entrepreneurship Development in Co-operative Sector

Entrepreneurship development deals with human resources, motivation, skills, competencies, social and economic risks. It develops entrepreneurs through systematic Entrepreneurship Development Programmes and developing the core business. In a country like India with growing unemployment, the co-operative sector can promote industrial co-operatives, tiny and small industries, agricultural and non-agricultural activities, farm and non-farm activities. For these, they need entrepreneurship culture and spirit. The prevalence of educated unemployed youth, can be involved in the culture of co-operative entrepreneurship and the spirit will eventually grow. In areas such as IT and computerisation young people can enter into entrepreneurship. Tamilnadu is blessed with self-financing institutions/colleges which are churning out computer engineers etc. therefore they can form viable cooperative ventures dealing with professional fields i.e., cooperative internet, cooperative browsing centres etc.

Again, the local indigenous entrepreneurship can be tapped and used by the new generation co-operatives (NGC's). All these can be possible through new perspective and approaches such as (1) Effective and efficient training (2) Consultancy (3) Motivation and use of encouragement techniques (4) Development of management skill programmes (5) Creation of awareness (6) Use of entrepreneurship development programmes (EDPs) through reputed institutions and centre for entrepreneurship development (CED) (7) Targeting the right groups such as, technical employees, young engineers, traders, artisans/craftsmen. In fact, Tamil Nadu State is among the leading states in turning out qualified engineers and technicians. They can be urged or motivated to create cooperative enterprises such as Cooperative Website creation etc.,

Constraints Affecting and Confronting Co-operative Entrepreneurship

The co-operative institutions must motivate and stimulate the culture of entrepreneurship in the co-operative system itself. They must engage the EDP offered by specialised agencies. However, there are a number of constrains and problems which are affecting co-operative entrepreneurship and few are mentioned here below:

(1) Insufficient industrial and market information. (2) Inadequate technological knowledge and skills. (3) Ineffective infrastructure. (4) Lack of start-up capital and low capital base. (5) Lack of business planning skills. (6) Lack of capital for expansion and modernisation. (7) Illiteracy (men and women). (8) Inadequate infrastructure facilities i.e., industrial sheds (9) Lack of managerial skill to start and manage the enterprise. (10) Lack of risk taking ability. (11) Not sure of sustained support. (12) They are economically and politically weak. (13) Low access to support system and business services i.e. computer services, information processing services, R and D, marketing services, human development services. (14) Constraints of quality of human resources. (15) Low lobbying capacity. (16) They are affected by globalisation and liberalisation policies, including unilateral liberalisation. (17) Multilateral trading rules under agreements of world trading (WTO). (18) Affected by liberalisation of services/infrastructure i.e., exogenous forces influencing co-operative entrepreneurship.

Strategies for Enhancing and Developing Co-operative Entrepreneurship

A number of strategies have been attempted by the author to ensure that co-operative entrepreneurship is made competent in the liberalised economy. This strategies will enhance and develop cooperative entrepreneurship in the long-run. A few of the strategies are:

(1) *Entrepreneurial hybridisation strategy:* The hybrid element in co-operatives refers to co-partnership within the co-operative sector or alliance aspect with other sectors in the economy and with inter-co-operative relations. The co-operative sector can associate itself with private and public sector units for promotion of business, improve their managerial skills and increase investment. The inter-co-operative relationship and co-partnership of co-operative sector are essential for entrepreneurship growth and development. (2) *Co-operative metamorphosis:* Co-operative institutions must undergo thorough metamorphosis process in order to face new changes and challenges brought about by LPG's. In fact, they can capture the new opportunities brought about by the open market economy. It is only possible by incorporating the entrepreneruship culture and spirit in the co-operative sector. (3) The ability of the cooperative sector to effectively and efficiently manage the eight 'Ms' for better growth and enhanced enterprises development: While managing the co-operative enterprises the eight Ms' must be managed properly. These eight Ms' are (a) Men (b) Materials (c) Machine (d) Methods (e) Milieu (environment) (f) Measurement (g) Money and (h) Markets. In addition to these, the co-operative entrepreneurial qualities are essential. The co-operative entrepreneurship requires certain specific qualities traits and aptitude for the efficient use of the eight Ms'. These could be initiative and independence, industries, co-operation, ability to learn, ability to work, team spirit, leadership skill, communication skills and negotiation skills, capacity to analyse, commitment and conviction, risk taking co-operators must be hopeful about future and search for new environment, high personal efficiency, morality, use time management techniques, business acumen, self-confidence perseverance, and quick decision making process. (3) A strategy to develop cooperative members interest in entrepreneurship and promote self-awareness in cooperative members. (4) Expand the role of support organisation. (5) Access to adequate funds and financial support (low rate of interest). (6) Developing business planning managerial capacity. (7) Improving marketing operations and marketing

management. (8) Develoment of technological capabilities. (9) Modernisation of machines and equipments. (10) National and State Policy support. (11) Provision of consultancy services. (12) Provision of training and education in co-operative entrepreneurships. (13) Undertaking research and development (product and processes development). (14) Business and economic diversification. (15) Suitable Balance between business transactions and cultural practices.

To sum up, a modified Chinese quotation would deem fit which goes like this "If you give a poor man fish his immediate problem of hunger may be satisfied. But, if you teach him fishing, he will be a co-operative entrepreneur and get out of socio-economic-poverty problems permanently".

Notes and References

1. Agarwal A.K. (1975) "Initiative, enterprise and economic choice in India- A study of pattern on entrepreneurship in India", Munshiram Manoharlal, New Delhi.
2. Burrows. D. (1983) "The Development of Small Business in the Pacific; Problems and Solutions" INA speech series No. 22.
3. Capati. A.P. (1985) "Cross-cultural Characteristics of the Entrepreneur" Entrepreneurial Development and Small Industry Stimulation in Developing Countries.
4. Drucke Peter. F. (1985) "Innovation and Entrepreneurship" Harper and Row.
5. El-Namaki. M.S.S (1988) "Encouraging Entrepreneurs in Developing Countries" Long Range Planning, XXIV No. 4.
6. Flahvin. A (1985) "Why Small Business Fail" Australian Accountant-LV-9.
7. Government of India (2000) 1999-2000 Ministry of Finance, Economic Division, New Delhi.
8. Government of India (2000), "WTO and Its Implication for Industry" Office of the Economic Adviser, Ministry of Commerce and Industry.
9. Hailey J.M. (1986) "Small Indigenous Business in the Pacific" International Small Business Journal V-1.
10. J.S.Canol (1986) "Entrepreneurship and Indigenous business in the Republic of the Marshall Islands, Honolulu East-West Centre.
11. Karmer H.E and Herbig P.A (1994) "Cultural Differences in doing Business, Germany and the South Pacific" Review of Business.

12. Kilby. P. (1971) "Entrepreneurship and Economic Development", Free Press, New York.

13. Mathur, Sathish B (1999) "Sickness in Small Scale Sector—Causes and Cure with Special Reference to the Role of Commercial Banks" Concept Publishing Company, New Delhi.

14. Mukherjee Neela (2000) "World Trade Organisations and India's Trade Policy in Services, Vikas Publishing House, New Delhi.

15. Plotkin H.M., (1990) "Portrait of Successful Small Business Owners" Small Business Reports XV-1.

16. Richard Lynn (1973) "The Entrepreneur Case Studies", George Allen and Unwin Ltd, London.

17. T. Venkateswar Rao and Uday Pareekh (1978) "Developing Entrepreneurship—A Handbook Learning System" New Delhi.

18. Vasant Desai (1990) "Entrepreneurial Development and Management", Himalaya Publication.

19. Vasant Desai (1998) "Dynamics of Entrepreneurial Development and Management" Himalaya Publishing House, New Delhi.

17

Decorticating Industries in Theni District—A Study

*Mrs. A. Mary Grace**
*Mr. S. Amivthaiyan***
*Dr. S. Maria John****

Growth of Small Scale Industries in India is a significant feature of the Indian Economy. The Small Scale sector covers wide range of activities. It is also playing a pivotal role in employment generation with low capital investment. At present it has provided employment opportunities to around 18 million people. The Government of India, recognising the importance and role of rural industries, has been allocating large amounts during all the plan periods.

Table 1 provides the plan outlays during the plan periods (vide Table 1). In India small scale industries include traditional and modern small industries, cottage industries, tiny units, business and industry related services etc. Consequent to the provisions during the plan periods, there

* Mrs. A. Mary Grace, Lecturer (SG) History, J.A. College for Women, Periyakulam 625 601, Theni Dt. Tamil Nadu.
** Mr. S. Amivthaiyan, Lacturer (SG) Commerce, St. Jude's College, Thuthur, K.K.Dt., Tamil Nadu.
*** Dr. S. Maria John, Reader in Commerce, Research Advisor and Supervisor, (Madurai Kamaraj University and Manonmoniam Sundaranar University), C.P.A. College, Bodi-625 513.

has been tremendous growth of small and Rural Industries (vide Table 2).

Table 1
Plan outlays for Rural Industrialisation

Sl. No.	*Plan Period*	*Outlays Rs. In Crores*	*Cumulative Percentage*
1.	First Plan	42	0.34
2.	Second Plan	187	1.86
3.	Third Plan	241	3.81
4.	Annual Plan	126	4.83
5.	Fourth Plan	293	7.20
6.	Fifth Plan	592	11.99
7.	Sixth Plan	1780	26.41
8.	Seventh Plan	2753	48.70
9.	Eight Plan	6334	100.00
	Growth rate in percentage	15081	-

Growth rate is calculated as yt/yo x 100

Table 2
Growth of Small and Rural Industries
(1980-81 to 1998-99)

Period	*No. of Units (In Lakhs)*	*Production (Rs In Crores)*	*Employment (In Lakhs)*	*Exports (Rs In Crores)*
1980-81	4.48	28060	71.0	1643
1984-85	8.50	50520	90.0	2580
1988-89	11.59	106400	113.0	5490
1992-93	22.35	209300	134.0	17785
1996-97	28.57	412636	160.0	39249
1998-99	31.21	538357	175.2	57488

Cottage Industries as feeder units to other industrial units, are mostly managed by artisans and skilled craftsman and are involved in traditional activities such as agriculture, khadi, handlooms, handicrafts etc. These are generally associated with part time or full time occupations in rural and semi urban areas utilising locally available resources and or human skill.

Tiny Units are the enterprises having an investment limit of less than 5 lakhs, whereas ancillary units have Rs. 75 Lakhs. These ancillary units are engaged in manufacturing parts, components, sub assemblies, toolings or intermediaries rendering services to one or more industrial units. These also serve as supporting units to large industries. The small and tiny units account for 35 per cent of the gross value of the output in the manufacturing sector, about 80 per cent of the total industrial employment and about 40 per cent of the total exports of the country.

Service Establishments are units involved in all industry related service and business enterprises, irrespective of location with recognised potential for generating employment. The investment ceilings correspond to those of tiny units.

The Cottage Industries are more or less house hold industries depending on local resources catering only to a limited local market. These industries may be classified into:-

1. Part-time rural cottage industries
2. Whole-time rural industries and
3. Urban Cottage Industries.

The Part-time Rural Cottage Industries cover all such industries which provide supplementary occupation to agriculturists and which are mostly processing industries, agro based industries, fruit and vegetable preservation and utilisation, handloom weaving, tadi, palm gur jaggary making and basket and rope making etc.

This study relates in general to groundnut industries which are agro-based processing industries. Groundnut is used in two types of village industries. They are:

1. Groundnut decorticating industries and
2. Oil industries

In a decorticating industry groundnut is processed, i.e., the outer shell or covering is removed. This decortication is done by machines by employing some persons in the premises of the entrepreneur. The other activities included in processing groundnut are drying, storing, packing etc. This processed kernel is sold to the following: (vide Table 3).

Table 3
Pattern of Distribution of Processed Nut by Entrepreneurs

Sl. No.	Category	Percentage
1.	Small business people	16%
2.	Other business people	38%
3.	Wholesalers	14%
4.	Oil industries direct cottage	15%
5.	Large oil units-own	17%

1. Small business people i.e., those who carry on cottage business at their homes.
2. Other business people i.e., those who carry on provision type of business.
3. Wholesalers who deal only in kernel business and
4. Sent to oil industries (Cottage) and
5. Large oil units

Oil Industries indulge in extracting oil from the processed kernel. These industries take oil not only from groundnut but also from other types of dals and seeds. The reason behind this is that of inconsistency in supply of groundnut to these entrepreneur. They get cake too which is sold separately.

Oil industries are of two types, They are:

1. Oil industries carrying on business at large scale and
2. Oil industries which are carried on at very small scale i.e. this type of industries are run either at the own residence of the entrepreneur or at a small

hired place and employing a very few workers. They use one or two machines. These people extract oil from various dals and nuts.

This research was carried on in Aundipatti Taluk (Theni District—Tamil Nadu) which consists of many types of industries (vide Table 4) and nearly 20 groundnut industries. These industries comprise both decorticating and oil industries. Theni District has 5 Taluks viz. Aundipatti, Bodinayakanur, Uthamapalayam, Periyakulam and Theni.

Table 4
Factories and Industries Located in Theni District

Sl. No.	*Nature*	*Number*
1.	Registered working factories	301
2.	Large scale industries	18
3.	Medium scale industries	12
4.	Small scale industries	582
5.	Cottage industries	182
6.	Unregistered cottage units	NA

In all the Taluks there has been groundnut production every year. During some years the production in one Taluk exceeds the production of the other Taluk. Among all the Taluks, the production of groundnut in Aundipatti Taluk, often exceeds the production of other Taluks, has three significances viz.

(a) Large production in quantity

(b) Large production in quality (size of the nut) and

(c) More oil content.

The nature of the soil of Aundipatti and the climatic conditions have proved more productivity of groundnut in the locality As there is more demand for the groundnut cultivated in and around Aundipatti Taluk, this area has been selected for the study. On the basis of the maximum turnover of groundnut in the industries of the sample area, 10 industries

(5 decorticating industries and 5 oil industries) were selected and a survey has proved that the sample respondents have been facing many problems in connection with handling of the kernel.

The very object of the study is to probe into the various problems (both economical and technological) faced by the respondents and to suggest to possible recommendations that require immediate action.

Findings of the Study

Shortage of Raw Materials

The cottage worker suffers from acute shortage of raw material. The groundnut industry is wholly dependent upon the supply of raw groundnut. The groundnut growers are unable to supply the nut, throughout the year, to the industries, as this crop is seasonal. Hence the shortage of raw groundnut is always felt. In the study area there are two types of industries viz.

(*a*) Industries at large scale of operation

(*b*) Industries at low scale of operations.

The industries which indulge in huge business operations are rightly categorised as healthy business enterprises. They buy more raw materials, produce more, sell more and enjoy more. They also procure and hoard groundnut in bulk and operate the market. The average industries and low scale operating industries have to depend largely on the market operators. They fix the price of the groundnut (raw materials) and act as middlemen in the field. Thus the artisan does not get enough of what he wants, what he gets is of poor quality and that too has to be bought at higher price.

Lack of Credit and Finance

The financial disability of small artisans is beyond doubt. Their financial needs consists of the purchase of raw materials, working expenses and accommodation between production and sale of the products. The internal sources are quite inadequate. This leads to instability of their profits which deters banks from giving unsecured loans. Their requirements are met by village money lenders who charge usurious rate of interest. The total amount of loan granted to them by the commercial banks forms a very small part of the total loans to the industry.

Low Level of Technology and Skill

The development of the village and small scale industries is hampered by the present low level of technology and shortage of trained and experienced supervisory personnel. So that the methods and art of production technique especially the producers for want of information, know very little about modern technologies which have revolutionsed production in small units in advanced countries. There is little research and development in this field in the country.

Competition from Large Scale Industries

Large scale industries, organised as they are on modern lines, using latest production technology and having access to many facilities can easily outsell the small producers. The small producers cannot therefore, stand up against them in the market.

Sickness and Inefficiency

Quite a large proportion of small industries has fallen sick. Their number run into lakhs. At present as many as 2.96 lakhs units are sick. This is exclusive over a lakh sick units which are not traceable or are not in existence. The reason for such sickness is that in many of the units 45 per cent to 60 per cent of its capacity remains unutilised. The reason may be incompetent manager, improper location, insufficient technology, skill, inadequate infrastructure facilities etc.

Inadequate Cost Analysis

Inadequate product-cost analysis blinds entrepreneurs to the losses incurred by adding new products willy-nilly. As the sample members deal with many products viz coconut, neem seed, gingely seed etc. they could not calculate the cost per product. Usually, there are one or more products or product lines that should be dropped.

Another common failing is gearing the operations to the income statement and ignoring the other financial statements. Lack of concern with cash flow and the productivity of capital employed can be fatal to the small company that is on its own. Entrepreneurs can make better use of the funds which they already have by making use of financial statements rather than seeking for new funds. Thus entrepreneurs need to realise that the surest test of their business success is sufficient and profits growing from year to year.

Cost of Electricity

Separation of oil and cake from the concerned raw materials requires the use of machineries. Machines, now-a-days are not operated by men, but by electricity. The cottage entrepreneur, who uses machineries, are charged the commercial rate (Rs. 3.20 per unit) by the electricity boards. This is a great burden to these small entrepreneurs which prevent their growth and expansion.

Collection of Debts

A businessman cannot depend only on cash sales. He has to depend on credit sales too. Credit sales is profitable as well as a risky affair. Most of the entrepreneurs face the problem of debt collection. It has been proved that there has been an average of 25 per cent bad debts on credit sales which is made to small house hold businessmen this occurrence of bad debts is due to the downfall of small cottage units, diversification of business (change of business) loss in business, family commitments, etc.

No business can operate without inventories. It needs protection. Guarding inventory thus becomes essential and forms strength to the unit.

Inventory comes in various forms such as supplies, raw materials, goods in process of manufacture, finished goods and floor stock (display).

It is always prudent to guard inventory as well as the inventories cost money in several ways.

Groundnut occupies a vast floor area. So a business man has to allocate a major portion of the industry for keeping the raw groundnut, semi-finished and finished stock. Maintenance of the whole area for keeping of the goods results ultimately in high cost.

Groundnut production is purely seasonal. So a large volume of raw groundnut is to be preserved till it is used in the process of production. The harvesting season lasts just for 2 months only. So the businessmen dealing in groundnut have to invest a lot in procuring raw groundnut. As, with in a short period, their raw groundnut has to be procured for storing, the businessmen are unable to generate the fund from their own business. Hence they borrow. Thus by this process money is tied up. This tie up money causes payment of interest.

Raw groundnut has to be stored for a very long time in the factory. So risk is more in preservation. So to get rid of from the risk, the entire stock is insured. Insurance in this respect is considered to be costly as premium is paid on the basis of the area of storage.

Storage is done in large areas. Hence it is bound to pay property tax on them. Cost of protection from pilferage and weather, pests and insects also cause damage. So to destroy them some cost is incurred.

Marketing Problem

Marketing the groundnut oil is the major problem faced by the small and large entrepreneurs. The sample members are of the opinion that, if at all they could sell one kilogram of groundnut oil at least for Rs. 40, it will be of benefit to them. At this situation, it is very difficult, if not impossible, to sell them at this required price. It is due to the Globalisation policy of the government (bilateral agreement) As the price of groundnut oil is more, consequently the demand decreases. Another reason for such a fall in demand for this oil is that of the import of palmoline (Palmoil) by the government even at Rs. 21 per litre. So the middle income group as well as the people below and at poverty line switch on to the substitute. At present the price of Gingely oil has also fallen down to a certain extent.

Suggestions

There are many problems which stand as an obstacle on the improvement of groundnut industry. In this study the problems with regard to inventories are mostly highlighted and some suggestions for optimising the inventory have been made.

The businessmen can opt for a nearby source of supply that gives prompt delivery too. The supplier may be asked to carry the inventory. Sometimes one may charge for transportation. But this arrangement will save lot of money tied up in long-term inventory.

When suppliers offer quantity discounts one must see that the savings is not off set by other costs. One can negotiate a year's supply in order to get quantity discounts, then demand that the goods be supplied in small quantities as and when one needs them.

One can look for faster quick and cheaper transportation modes. It is better to keep the inventory only as finished goods. One can expand the concept of time. If it takes six weeks for delivery one does not need a six-week supply, as one can order smaller quantities for weekly or daily delivery.

The businessmen have to shop around for best price and group purchase are suggested. In case a rented warehouse is established by the supplier one can prefer such a supplier.

Other Suggestions for Improvement

It has been found that large scale industries dominate the market and they do not allow the small industries to come up. Purchase of raw materials can be made on co-operative basis. Regulated markets functioning in the districts can also render services of this nature.

The civil supplies corporation can establish warehouses to preserve groundnut at a very meager rate of Rent to the agricultural farmers. Revolving credit facility system could be followed in this connection and commercial banks can give guarantee to the suppliers who extend revolving credit system. Electricity can be supplied at a concessional rate. Subsidy may be granted to the cultivators which may reduce the cost of production in total.

The Government can allot more funds towards Research and Developments in the field of agriculture in general and commercial oil seed crops in particular. Western pattern of production (cultivation) could be introduced by the Department of Agriculture in every district by selecting unemployed graduates who have at least little property for cultivation. Co-operative farming to a certain extend can also be thought of with the help of establishing cooperative societies in the regard. Training the graduates can be imparted at a low cost quickly.

The idle decorticating machines available in the co-operative societies can be made good by the Government of Tamilnadu which will be of much benefit to the poor entrepreneurs.

The impact, on implementation of the above said suggestion may be that, there will be more employment generation, more benefit to the agriculturists and entrepreneurs, and more income to the nation. This may also prove that the rural area itself will get develop economically and socially.

References

1. Agarwal AN Indian Economy, Problems of Development and Planning, 21st Edition-Wishwa Prakashan 1995.
2. Entrepreneurship Development, Centre for Research and Industrial Staff Performance Bhopal. TATA MC Grawhill Publishing Co. Ltd., New Delhi.
3. Memoria CB and Tripathi B.B. Agricultural Problems of India, Kithab Mahal, Allahabad, 1997.
4. District Profile, Department of Statistics, Theni District.
5. Small Industries Development Organisation and Eight Five Year Plan 1992-97 and 1998-99.
6. State Directories of Industries, Government of Tamilnadu-Chennai.

18

Impact of WTO on Rural Small Entrepreneur in India

*Dr. V. Selvaraj**

The importance of dairy in the Indian Economy can be gauged from the fact that milk is the single largest item, which is estimated to fetch Rs. 450 billion way ahead of rice and wheat. The estimated value of the animals alone is around Rs. 35 billion. Dairy animals also contribute to hides/skins and dung valued at Rs. 60 billion. Dairy sector provides additional income and generates job opportunities for 80 million farmer families. More than 70% of marginal farmers and landless labour maintain dairy animals to supplement their income. Women contribute 71% of the labour force to dairy as compared their share of 33% in crop farming. India now stands number one in milk production in the world. There are more than 97,000 milk co-operative societies in 264 districts as per AMUL pattern and at present this sector grows at the rate of 6.5% per annum. Millions of entrepreneur is doing dairy as business. With the advent of liberalisation and move towards globalisation, Indian economic environment offers challenge to entrepreneurs, who are involving in dairy industry.

Dairy is one of the sectors affected by WTO. During the negotiations in 1985, we failed to bargain and agree to allow

* Dr. V. Selvaraj, Reader in Commerce, Nehru Memorial college, Puthanampatti-621 007. Trichy, Tamil Nadu.

import of milk and milk products under zero per cent bound duty. In 1999, Indian traders imported 10,000 metric tones of milk powder and in 2000, we were threatened by the arrival of fresh milk in Mumbai from New Zealand at the landed cost Rs. 9. Fortunately, the Government of India in its budget of 2001 has imposed heavy duty on milk and the problem has been halted temporarily. This duty will have to be abolished before the year 2006, as per the WTO agreement. Hence we have 3 years to gear ourselves for international competition. This is probably the last chance for rural entrepreneurs to organise themselves and convert this challenge into an opportunity.

High Cost of Milk Production

What are our problems? Why are we threatened by the international dairy market? The main problems are high cost of milk production, high cost on milk processing, marketing and poor quality milk due to unhygienic milk handling. Hence we need to address these problems on priority. The cost of milk production in India is high because the average milk yield of Indian cows is only 978 Kg as compared to 6273 Kg in Denmark, 5289 Kg in France, 5462 Kg in United Kingdom, 5938 Kg in Canada, 7038 Kg in USA and 11000 Kg in Israel. The weather condition in Israel are worse than India. The temperature in summer exceeds 47°C-48°C; while the temperature in winter is as low as 4°c-5°c. In spite of such bad weather and severe water shortage, the average milk production of dairy cows is 11000 Kg/Lactation. Hence, there is good scope for more quantity of milk production per cow is possible in India.

High Cost on Milk Handling

Our dairy entrepreneurs get about Rs. 7-8 per at their village co-operative. This milk is handled at several levels by Co-operative or private till it reaches the main dairy located in a large city for pasteurisation. The milk is then sent to consumers through various outlets. In this process, the consumers have to pay almost twice the farmgate price i.e. around Rs. 14-16. The present system is not only unhygienic but also expensive. There is good scope for reducing the number of agencies handling the milk to reduce the cost on handling.

Strategy for Conversion of Challenge Into Opportunity

Reduction in Cost of Milk Production

It is necessary to immediate steps to reduce the cost of milk production by increasing the productivity of our animals. Animal Husbandry Department should assist the rural small entrepreneurs (Farmers) in solving their problem time to time. Concurrent with improving genetic potential of dairy animals, necessary nutrient input has to be provided for maximising the dairy production. Our Indian milk producers should try to get more quantity of milk per cow as like Israel milk producer. Production of more quantity of milk per cow will bring down the cost of production. More quantity of milk production per cow has been achieved through proper housing, feed and water management, apart from superior quality germplasm.

Reduction of Milk Handling Cost by Setting up of Direct Marketing Association with E-Commerce Facility

Rural small entrepreneur is also necessary to look for an alternative model of milk processing and selling. They should create Direct Marketing Association at the levels of village, union and district. The DMA will set up processing and retail outlet for local needs. It should sell fresh milk as well as value added items such as milk cream, condensed milk, dried milk, malted milk, cultured milk, filled milk, butter, margarine cheese and ice-creams. These items can be sold in local markets and also exported to foreign countries through internet and E-Commerce. Why should a rural small entrepreneur come to town to sell his produce? E-commerce today provides the infrastructure to communicate and share information, between the buyers and sellers. Infotech is at the heart of marketing today. Information is extensively used to discover new markets and newer ways of marketing. E-commerce basically involves using a combination of intranet and Internet to link sellers, suppliers, distributors, banks and customers where information exchange, price negotiation, order placements, delivery confirmation, billing and payments take place-online. It is essentially an evolving set of IT tools and implementation techniques, as well as the business strategies and practice necessary to do business electronically.

Internet solution companies assist to design website for you. They do services of Domine Registration, Web Design and Development and Hoisting. DMA should get website address by paying of appropriate fees to internic institution. The rural small entrepreneur can not get website address due to lack of funds, professionalism, Internet etc. All rural small entrepreneur should become a member in the Direct Marketing Association. Those who are members in this association can utilise the available facility of e-commerce. It is enough to have an e-mail address for individeual small rural entrepreneurs. They can link themselves to Direct Marketing Association Website through their e-mail address. Both the central and state governments, Voluntary Organisation, Self Help Group and Enthusiastic computer learned entrepreneurs should come forward to setup Direct Marketing Association with e-commerce facility. This will definitely reduce the cost on handling.

With reduction in the cost of milk production and cost on milk handling, the retail price can be reduced significantly and this can help the rural small entrepreneurs face the challenge of imported milk. The rural small entrepreneurs can send their dairy products to any corner of the world. (International Market). Threat from the WTO will be converted into an opportunity by the rural small entrepreneur through the minimisation of cost of production and cost on handling of dairy products.

19

Rural Employment Opportunities in Khadi and Village Industries

*Dr. V. Madasamy**

*A. Joseph Xavier***

Village industries are playing a key role in the industrialisation of rural area in India. It provides maximum job to rural people with locally available materials. In this paper an attempt has been made to study the problems of rural entrepreneurs and employment opportunities available in Khadi and Village Industries in particular.

Rural Entrepreneur

A rural entrepreneur is an entrepreneur who forms an industrial unit and works in it in the rural area.

Problems of Rural Entrepreneurs

In rural areas, the entrepreneurs are facing the following problems like:

- Lack of finance
- Shortage of raw materials

* Dr. V. Madasamy, M. Com., M. Phil., Ph. D, Reader in Commerce, Ayya Nadar Janaki Ammal College, Sivakasi-626 124.

** A. Joseph Xavier, M. Com., M. Phil., B. Ed, PGDCA., Research Scholar, Department of Commerce, Ayya Nadar Janaki Ammal College, Sivakasi-626 124.

- Lack of market coverage
- Lack of technical/managerial skills
- Improper project planning
- Shortage of power
- Lack of transport/communication facilities
- Lack of research and development facilities

Several steps are taken by both the Central and State Governments to promote entrepreneurship in rural areas through various financial institutions and organisations. Khadi and Village Industries Commission is one of the organisations for developing entrepreneurship in rural areas in particular.

The next part of this paper is focusing on the potentialities of employment opportunities available in Khadi and Village Industries in particular.

Khadi and Village Industries Commission (KVIC)

The KVIC is a statutory body created by an Act of Parliament (No. 61 of 1956 and as amended by Act No. 12 of 1987). Established in April 1957, it took over the work of the former All India Khadi and Village Industries Board with the primary objective of developing rural employment opportunities.

Objectives

The broad objectives that the KVIC set before it are;

1. The social objective of providing employment.
2. The economic objective of producing saleable articles and
3. The wider objective of creating self-reliance amongst the poor and building up of a strong rural community sprit.

Its wide range of activities includes;

(i) Training of artisans

(ii) Extension of assistance for procurement of raw materials

(iii) Marketing of finished goods

(iv) Arrangement for manufacturing and distribution of improved tools, equipment and machinery to procure on concessional terms.

KVIC and Rural Employment Opportunities

The Khadi and Village Industries Commission (KVIC) has been playing a very important role in generating large-scale employment in the rural areas with low per capita investment. India can thrive only if its' three forth population in the rural areas around 5.80 lakhs villages survive. Hence the relevance of Khadi and Village Industries in the rural economy in today's context is an important one as ever in the past.

Rural Employment Generation Programme (REGP)

In order to develop Khadi and Village Industries for (KVIs) for generation of additional employment for 2 million persons as recommended by the High Power Committee (HPC) under the chairmanship of the then Prime Minister in 1994, the KVIC has launched a programme known as the Rural Employment Generation Programme (REGP.) In addition to the normal programmes, some of the special programmes also have been started and subsequently they have been merged with normal programmes. These special programmes were:-

(a) District Special Employment Programme (SEP)

(b) 125 Block Development Programme (BDP)

(c) National projects on selected village industries viz. Beekeeping, Leather and Pottery etc.

The programme of KVIC has been implemented covering already in about 2.70 lakhs villages benefiting number of rural artisans/entrepreneurs especially large number of women folk, SC/ST and other weaker sections. Among the various programmes of KVIC, REGP is very much in the limelight, with Government of India laying great hopes on Khadi and

Village Industries sector to remove the severe unemployment problem in rural areas of the country.

The KVIC has announced a special margin money scheme to boost rural economy by creating job opportunities in rural areas.

Margin Money Scheme (MMS)

(a) Eligible Projects

The scheme is applicable to all new village industry projects set up in "Rural Areas".

Rural Area

"Rural Area" means, the area comprised in any village and includes the area comprised in any town, the population of which does not exceed 20,000 as per latest census or such other figure as the Central Government may specify from time to time and any area classified as village as per revenue records of the State/U.T. irrespective of population.

Village Industry

"Village Industry" means any industry located in rural areas, which produces any goods or renders any services with or without the use of power and in which fixed amount per head of any artisan or a worker does not exceed Rs. 50,000.

(b) Eligible Activities

All eligible 120 activities under KVIC as well as those, which do not appear in the negative list, circulated by KVIC are eligible for financing under the scheme.

The 120 activities are categorised under seven heads. They are:

Negative List

The negative list includes, Manufacturing of Polythene carry bags of less than 20 microns thickness and manufacture of carry bags or containers made of recycled plastics for storing, carrying dispensing or packaging of foodstuff and any other item, which causes environmental problems.

S. No.	Heads	No. of Industries
1.	Mineral Based Industry	15
2.	Forest Based Industry	12
3.	Agro Based Industry	21
4.	Polymer and Chemical Based Industry	13
5.	Engineering and Non-conventional energy	25
6.	Textile Industry	14
7.	Service Industry	20
	Total	120

Source: KVIC Dairy-2002.

(c) Eligible Borrowers and Ceiling Limit

The rural entrepreneurs eligible under this scheme are:

(i) Individual (Artisans/Entrepreneurs—projects upto a ceiling limit of 10.00 lakhs)

(ii) Institutions, Co-operative Societies, Trusts.

The following persons are not eligible to get the Margin Money Scheme.

Partnership firms, Private/Public Limited Companies, Joint Venture, Co-obligators or HUF.

The Margin Money Scheme envisages that;

(i) 25% of the project cost for the projects upto Rs. 10.00 Lakhs will be provided as "Margin Money" by way of middle end subsidy.

(ii) For projects above Rs. 10.00 lakhs and upto Rs. 25.00 lakhs, rate of Margin Money will be 25% of the project cost upto Rs. 10.00 lakhs plus 10% of the remaining cost of the project.

(iii) In the case of weaker section beneficiary viz. SC/ ST/OBC/Women/Physically Handicapped/ex-servicemen and Monitory Community beneficiary/ institution and for hill, border and tribal areas, North Eastern Region, Sikkim, Andaman and

Nicobar Islands, Laksdweep, Margin money grant will be at the rate of 30 per cent of the project cost upto Rs. 10.00 lakhs and above this amount upto Rs. 25.00 lakhs, it will be 10% of the remaining cost.

(d) Borrower's Contribution

Under the scheme, the borrower is required to invest his "Own Contribution" of 10 per cent of the project cost. In case of SC/ST/OBC/women/Physically Handicapped/Ex-servicemen and Monitory Community and other weaker section borrowers, the contribution is 5 per cent of the project cost.

The maximum permissible limit for the own contribution is 50 per cent of the total project cost.

(e) Quantum of Loan

Banks will sanction 90 per cent of the project cost in case of general category borrower and 95 per cent of the project cost in case of weaker section beneficiary/Institution and disburse full amount of the loan.

Further, to increase the employment opportunities in rural areas KVIC is providing training on various Village Industries activities through various centers all over India.

Training Centres in Tamilnadu

The following Training Centres are providing training in Tamilnadu.

1. Khadi Gramodyog Vidyalaya, Veerapandi, Tirupur-Coimbatore District.
2. Dr. J.C. Kumarappa Institute of Rural Technology, T. Kallupatti, Madurai.
3. Central Palmgur and Palm Products Institute Madavaram, Chennai provides training especially on Palm Gur and other palm products industries.

For example Dr. J.C. Kumarappa Institute of Rural Technology, T. Kallupatti, Madurai is providing training in the following Khadi and Village Industrial activities, which are more suitable to start rural Industries.

Details of Training Provided by the Dr. J.C. Kumarappa Institute of Rural Technology, T. Kallupatti, and Madurai

S. No.	*Nature of product manufacturing*	*Duration*
1.	Footwear and leather products	6 Months
2.	Washing and bathing soap	2 Months
3.	Rexine products	3 Months
4.	Detergent powder	2 Months
5.	Cleaning powder	1 Week
6.	White pencil	2 Weeks
7.	Screen printing	3 Months
8.	Pots made out of soil	2 Months
9.	Toys made out of soil	2 Months
10.	Binding works, file and paper cover	2 Months
11.	Food items like masala, pickles etc.	1 Month
12.	Motor rewinding	3 Months
13.	Steel furnitures	3 Months
14.	Two-wheeler mechanism	3 Months
15.	Servicing electronic and electrical items	4 Months
16.	Khadi products	9 Months
17.	Bio-fertilizers and vermin compost.	4 days

Training is given to all persons those who have completed secondary or higher secondary level education and with age group between 18 and 35. Separate hostel facility is also available for women trainees. Trained persons from these centers are mostly welcomed by all Khadi and Village Industries. Trainees are given training on matters like production method, Sarvodaya Philosophy and accounting methods etc., with very low amount of fee.

Conclusion

Even though the above scheme appears to be very easy and feasible, still, both Central and State Governments are introducing so many programmes to create and increase employment opportunities in rural areas. When the people participation is increased with Government hands than the existing level there is no doubt that India can reach the spur development in rural area at the expected level. Can participation increase?

20

Entrepreneurism in Co-Operatives

*P. Ravi**

Introduction

"Entrepreneur is one of the most important inputs in the economic development of a country or of regions within the country".[1] Economic growth and industrialisation is the possible by-product of entrpreneurship. Rural enterprise development has been considered as one of the solutions to the problem of unemployment and poverty.

Since independence, the Government policies, programmes and various schemes were targeted towards the welfare and development of rural people. But the success of various schemes implemented by the Government is very low. To overcome these shortcomings, the government should organise Entrepreneurship Development Programmes to the educated unemployed youths in all the panchayats covering all the villages in the country. The programme should create awareness and much confidence among youths particularly in rural area. Another important aspect of the government through its network is to analyse the impact of the entrepreneurship programme in rural areas at regular intervals.

* P. Ravi, Research Scholar, Department of Commerce, Madurai Kamaraj University Madurai. 625021.

Entrepreneur

"An Entrepreneur is one who perceived profit opportunities and initiated action to fill currently unsatisfied needs". –Kirzner (1985)

Entrepreneurship

"Entrepreneurship is an act of innovation that involves endowing existing resources with new wealth producing capacity'—Drucker (1985).

Co-operative Entrepreneurship

"Co-operative entrepreneurship refers to a process of action undertaken by a group of associated individuals to form own business, distribute profit among members and induce the habit of thrift and investment through self-help and mutual help". —T. Asokan.

Now-a-days, sole proprietor and partnership form of enterprises have many risks. So, co-operative entrepreneurship is the only powerful and recognised form of enterprise. In recent times, co-operative entrepreneurism becomes increasingly important as a socio-economic proportion paving way for the participation of weaker sections in industrial and allied activities.

The co-operative movement in India started towards the beginning of the twentieth century. It is more than eighty years old. In the early years of the twentieth century, co-operatives were mainly organised as a defensive organisation for dealing with problems of indebtedness. But now co-operative movement is a strong force in the state concerned as well as national economy.

As per the Acts and Rules, no co-operative society/ enterprise shall be registered which does not consist of at least ten persons who have attained the age of majority.[2]

According to Sec. 3(1) of the Self-Help Co-operative Bill. 2001, the individuals ten in number from different ten families can get together and take decision for the formation of a co-operative society/enterprise for their socio-economic and cultural upliftment if they intend. "No outsiders force is there for such get together. They are empowered to frame the article of association for their own proposed co-operative society/enterprise as promoter and send the required papers such as memorandum of association which contains the proposed name of the co-operative society/enterprise. The address where the registered office of the co-operative society/enterprise to be situated, the objective of the co-operative enterprise, declaration of their promoters of their commitment to the co-operative principles. As provided a list of promoters with their complete address accompanied by the original articles of association and one true copy thereof, the proposed co-operative society/enterprise as adopted by the promoters and true copy of the resolution adopting the articles of association passed at a meeting by the signatories to such memorandum of association to the Registrar of Co-operatives by hand or by registered post for registration".[3]

The formation of a co-operative form of enterprises in rural areas is not an achievement. The real success of co-operative enterprises is governed by the co-operative strength in a dynamic business environment, i.e., making innovation, technological advancement and systematic commercialisation of the product or service with a focus on customer satisfaction and for the welfare of the society. But in most cases, co-operative enterprises have grown under the state patronage and protection. Most of the members of these enterprises are not having the basic knowledge about the business of their enterprises. They are members, that is all. A majority of the members think that they have no right to question any activities of the enterprise. To overcome all these shortcomings, the creation of a national network for the flow of vital information relating to the activities of the enterprises. The activities of the national network should be so designed as to enable members get motivated which increases the active participation in all the activities of the enterprises. This will promote the effective functioning of their enterprises.

The degree of member participation within any co-operative enterprise largely depends on the confidence built by the enterprise among its members. By such confidence, the member should think that the enterprise will help them to fulfill their goals included in the overall goal setting system of their co-operative enterprise.

The members should be rewarded in someway or the other. This will go a long way in tuning and motivating the effective participation of the members.

"The enterprise should recognise and ensure that the members should gain status, recognition through participation in the management of the enterprise".[4]

The co-operative form of enterprise may also be constituted for preserving the rain water, to manage the scarce natural resources and optimum utilisation of those resources for sustainable development. It is only possible in the village, if they function under the association or enterprise formed by themselves.

Traditionally, various groups are functioned at least one in every village. But they are not legally constituted and unauthorised. Because, they are illiterates, they are only having the skill to do the works efficiently and quickly like paddy harvesting and other allied agricultural works. But these works are of seasonal nature. After these season, the group voluntarily dissolved without any legal formalities. At that time, the landlords and rich people engaged these groups in favour of themselves.

Recently, "the Government of Kerala has begun a programme for the registered unemployed (Kerala State Self Employment Scheme for the Registered Unemployed) in the year 1999".[5] Under this scheme, people are undertaking conventional imitative types of activities and facing failure within no time. Along with promoting self-employment, the registered job seekers can be motivated to form co-operative enterprises to undertake innovative agro-based industrial enterprises capable of generating large employment chances.

In Tamilnadu also, in consultation with the National Federation of Labour Co-operatives Ltd., the employment exchanges with their data base can motivate people to set up such type of enterprises in every Panchayat. The Employment Exchanges should provide training not only to the white collar job but also the skilled labours with modern technologies. After the successful completion of training, the qualified and like-minded job seekers should be motivated to join together to form a business of their choice under co-operative sector.

Now co-operative enterprises should equip themselves to face the new economic and political environment. They should do a lot of introspection and evolve ways and means to strengthen themselves organisationally and financially. The members dedication towards the enterprises, true participation in the economic transactions in their own organisation and self-decision making for fulfillment of common need will no doubt, keep the enterprise alive and flourish for days to come.

REFERENCES

1. P. Saravanavel, Entrepreneurial Development Principles, Policies and Programmes IInd Edition 1997.
2. D. P. Neb, "Active members participation—A Precondition for success of co-operative organisations", Co-operative Perspective, VOMNICOM, Pune-7, Vol. 33, No. 3, Oct.-Dec., 1998.
3. M. Soundarapandian, Rural Entrepreneurship Growth and Potential, Kanishka Publishers and Distributors, New Delhi.
4. P. Puyalvannan, "Approaches for Village Development: Experiences form Ralegan Siddhi Village", Co-operative Perspective VOMNICOM, Pune-7 Vol. 36, No. 2, July-Sep., 2001.
5. T. Asokan, "Co-operative Entrepreneurship: The Paradigm for job seekers in Kerala", Co-operative Perspective, VOMNICOM, Pune-7, Vol. 36, No. 3, Oct.-Dec., 2001.
6. Vasant Desai, "Entrepreneurship and Technology", Small Scale Industries, Vol. 10.

21

Entrepreneurship in Micro Enterprises

*G. Ganesan**

*Dr. Mohammad Jaffar***

Introduction

We are rich both in intellect and availability of natural resources but we were waiting for somebody to change our mindset but now time has come to change our mind set ourselves. To have that patriotism in us, to contribute our best in terms of our own technologies or even modified technologies adaptable to us for ultimately realising Adaptable Rural Technologies (ART), through the help of entrepreneur together with the help of the networking of national programme and obviously with clear techno-vision in order to meet global competition and improve the productivity of micro enterprises.

Entrepreneurship is something which every one of us may have in our system. Depending on the level of entrepreneurship and the right environment that needs to be created, some may have the skill of a scientist, some may have good entrepreneurship as a business person and yet some more may excel in finding new production techniques in order to achieve cost benefit and better productivity. But one thing

* G. Ganesan, Lecturer in Commerce, Periyar Arts College, Cuddalore-607 001, Tamil Nadu.

** Dr. Mohammad Jaffar, Reader in Commerce, HKRH College, Uttamapalayam. Tamil. Nadu.

common in all **these activities** is a sense of belonging and commitment to the profession and society. It is that entrepreneurship in us that is required for success in micro enterprises.

But in any kind of entrepreneurship, getting more from less either from a small, medium or large scale enterprise with ensured quality of the product with a total integrated approach and a firm eye on human resource management is critical for success.

Issues

In the present global environment, the importance of micro enterprises in the state's and India's economy is significant. Besides generating employment at the lowest capital cost, small units have been the only sector earning net foreign exchange, accounting as they do, for over 35% of India's exports. In addition, they supply quality inputs to medium and even large units, who therefore, focus on better value addition to their own activities. Therefore micro enterprises through effective entrepreneurship are a must in order to strengthen our economy in total. This paper addresses main activities that are required to strengthen the micro enterprises.

Objectives of the Study

1. To study the concept and functions of micro enterprises.
2. To measure the achievements of micro enterprises.
3. To know the required new manufacturing technologies of entrepreneurs in micro enterprises.
4. To give appropriate suggestions in order to overcome the difficulties of micro enterprises.

Micro Enterprises

Micro enterprises that have been functioning in our country can be divided into two major categories namely, agricultural enterprises and non-agricultural enterprises at micro level. Agricultural enterprises is defined by the CSO in such a way that the enterprises which are engaged in raising livestock, agricultural services, forestry and longing and fishing etc., but excludes agricultural production and plantation. The non-agricultural enterprises include manufacturing and the entire gamut of services including trading, restaurants, communications finance and transport.

According to the Economic Census conducted by the Central Statistical Organisation (CSO) over the years, the share of agricultural enterprises, both in terms of sheer number and by employment, is on the rise and on the other side; the proportion of non-agricultural enterprises is showing a declining trend. The fact that the share of these enterprises and the labour force employed in them is on the rise reflects a natural and diversification process into agro-related sectors through rural entrepreneurship.

Progress

Over the time period 1980-1998, the share of agricultural enterprises rose from about 12% to over 18%. During the same period, the share of non-agricultural enterprises fell from about 88% to 81%. In this category, the main loser was the rural manufacturing sector, its share declined from around 39% to 25%. On the whole, the growth rate of non-agricultural enterprises sharply declined from 2.35% in the eighties to 1.65% in the nineties. The main reason for the declining trend is the lack of innovative entrepreneurships in the manufacturing sector but effective entrepreneurship in agricultural enterprises. Hence, it is needed to implement latest technology in manufacturing sector also in order to develop rural economy through rural industrialisation at micro level.

Technology in the Manufacturing Sector

Technology in the manufacturing sector is related to a whole spectrum of fields namely materials, machinery and equipment, process, manufacturing systems, and quality system. New materials play a major part in product and process innovations. Production process, product cost and quality in the sector have been significantly influenced.

Further technology is changing the face of industry. A stage has already been reached in the Small and Medium Enterprises sector in which obsolete technology spells doom. The lower levels of technology, the greater are the chances of elimination. The imperatives of technology upgradation are, therefore, quite transparent. To be competitive price is very critical since the trend everywhere is to freeze. In an inflationary economy, price management is one of the greatest challenges before small and medium enterprises. Quite often, technology holds the key to solutions which involve improving productivity and quality.

Need for Strategic Thinking

Strategy is a game of mind. Strategic thinking involves evolving a long-term vision that would enable the entrepreneur to foresee the emerging patterns and to plan a proper position for himself. A mission for the enterprise has to be developed from the long-term vision. Detailed strategies would need to be evolved to accomplish the mission and they have to be reviewed in pursuit of continued relevance and adequacy in the changing market place.

1. *Entrepreneur's Mindset*

Underlying the entire process of technology upgradation for improving productivity and quality, there is one invisible factor which is the most important. It is the mindset of the entrepreneurs. The entrepreneur must develop a mindset that would not allow him to rest unless he keeps pace with changes in the domain of the enterprise. As an entrepreneurship process consists of a constant search for alternatives, a certain amount of risk taking, perseverance and attempt to identify and utilise opportunities for better rural development. In addition modern concepts such as Just-In-Time (JIT) manufacturing Kaizen and Activity-Based Costing (ABC) etc., adopted by the unit have yielded remarkable results in that unit.

Measures to Overcome Problems of Micro Enterprises

Efforts should be made sufficiently by setting up more agro and rural based enterprises and make use of locally available cheap but quality raw materials and steps have to be taken to introduce latest cost effective techniques for value addition to the existing raw materials.

Small-scale industrial development in rural areas must be linked with local resources and sufficient investment will have to be made in human capital in the form of skill development and skill to have an impact on the employment situation.

Facilities for provision of credit, crucial inputs and marketing will have to be organised. Further people who are engaged in rural industrialisation should face no problem in marketing and they should have fair return for their products.

Arrangements have to be made to secure foreign offer for their products since there has been globalised market environment prevailed.

Infrastructure is another important aspect for growth of any economic activity. Therefore, proper infrastructure must be built up to move things flexible.

The role played by the state and central Government and large number of micro and mega enterprises and the financiers and non-governmental agencies have all to be networked to achieve every thing at most success.

Conclusion

Poverty and large population are significant and persistent problems in rural India. To overcome these problems micro enterprises should be started in large number at rural and semi-urban levels. Instead of mass production, production by masses concept should be developed in order to provide wide employment opportunities. In addition, Information Technology plays a pivotal role in industries which is necessary to cut operation cost drastically and to ensure high speed in every activity. Hence, it is essential on the part of entrepreneurs to make use of such technology and reduce cost of production, improve productivity and ensure total quality in every aspect.

REFERENCES

1. Vasanth Desai, Entrepreneurship Development.
2. Gupta and Srinivasan, Entrepreneurship Development.
3. The Financial Express, various issues.
4. The Economic Times various issues.
5. Business Today various issues.

22

Cooperative Entrepreneurism

*Mrs. T. Saroja**

Introduction

Industrialisation is one of the important means to usher in a economic and social transformation in the developing countries like India. More so, when agriculture cannot sustain the burden of increasing population, it is the industry and services sector which have to shoulder the responsibility of sustaining and accelerating the pace of economic development. Industrialisation is indispensable for the survival and growth of an economy. The country is looking forward for more and more entrepreneurs to build a strong national economy.

The Concept of Entrepreneurship

The spirit of desire for achievement is the basis for entrepreneurship. So people involve themselves in some work or other, some work for others and some are self-employed. The people who work for themselves are called "Entrepreneurs". The word Entrepreneur is derived from the French word "Entreprendre" meaning "to undertake". The entrepreneur is thus a person who organises and manages an activity/organisation, undertaking the risks for fulfilling some of his needs.

* Mrs. T. Saroja M. Com. M. Phil, Head, Department of Commerce, NS College Theni 625531. Tamil Nadu.

Entrepreneurship is a purposeful activity indulged in initiating, promoting and maintaining economic activities for the production and distribution of wealth. The individual as an entrepreneur is a critical factor in economic development and an integral part of social-economic transformation. The basic concept of Entrepreneurship connotes effectiveness, an urge to take risks in the face of uncertainties and intuition (i.e.) a capacity of showing things in a way which afterwards proves to the true.

The basis objective of entrepreneurship development is to build up strong and promising cadres of entrepreneurs, from among Indian youth belonging to different segments of society, with the application of tools and mechanisms capable of identifying, motivating and sustaining entrepreneurship spirit in them.

The entrepreneur is willing to undertake investment activity in a competitive economy, take financial risks, all of which create wealth employment and new capital for further economic activity.

Entrepreneurship and Economic Development

Development of the economy in any form is the outcome of human activity. This activity in a man envisages three roles as an organiser, worker and as a user of goods produced. Of these, the role of man in organising the factors of production is very important. Entrepreneurship development is one of the essential factors contributing to the economic growth and employment generation in developing economies.

Schumpeter established a relationship between the entrepreneur and economic development. He considered Entrepreneurship as a key factor in economic development. According to him, Entrepreneur is an innovative agent, who introduces something new into the economy. There is a positive correlation between the presence of entrepreneurial element and economic development in a society.

Entrepreneurship and Cooperatives

The establishment and growth of cooperatives is

regarded as one of the social and cultural development as well as human advancement. A cooperative is generally viewed as a socio-economic organisation that can fulfill both social and economic objectives of its members and that has its member's interests truly at heart. A cooperative is based on certain values and principles of its own, which distinguish it from other forms of organisations. The very motto of cooperation "Each for all and all for each", signifies loyalty, trust, faith and fellowship.

A cooperative organisation is an association of persons who have voluntarily associated together to achieve a common economic goals through a democratically controlled process.

Likewise Entrepreneurship as an economic activity emerges and functions in sociological and cultural setting. It may be conceived as a creative activity, which is resulted because of the free choice of an individual or social group.

Entrepreneurs endowed with capability to perceive opportunities, organise resources and set up and run successful industrial units are not found adequate in numbers, and whatever is available is not evenly dispersed all over the country. It is time to convert job seekers into job providers so as to generate further employment opportunities.

Thus the cooperatives and entrepreneurship are activities which aim at economic development of a nation with freedom of choice of the persons associated in it and also formed in social and cultural setting.

Cooperative Entrepreneurism

The Indian scenario is changing fast with modernisation, urbanisation and development of education and business. Moreover the new era which was ushered in India after the policy launching of the new Economic Policy in August in 1991, is characterised by privatisation, liberalisation and globalisation, several structural and operational reforms have been introduced in Indian economy in this era and process of reforms still on with the advent of information technology. This resulted in increased competition among all sectors of the Indian economy i.e., public, private and cooperatives. The people involved in the cooperative sectors feels that they are competent to face the competitions form the public sector, but not from the private sector. Moreover the entrepreneurial competitancies of different persons may be more successful than the entrepreneurial traits of a single individual. Because the individual may not possesses all the traits and he look upon outsourcing of services in the form of consultancy etc.

So it is a high time to think over the structural and operational change in the sectors of our Indian economy. This will emerge the new concept of "Cooperative Entrepreneurism". Germany is well known for cooperative Entrepreneurism.

Strategies for Developing Co-Operative Entrepreneurism

Development of any Entrepreneurship confronts several problems may be of individual, group and institutional. It is an Individual who has to take the initiative to decide on starting and managing his activity/organisation. He also need the approval and support of his group. The individual and the group constitute the client system. The institution such as governmental and non-governmental agencies are to stimulate the client system towards entrepreneurial activity. Entrepreneurship development requires an environment in which an entrepreneur can learn and discharge his function. It is well recognised that entrepreneur are not born; they can be developed and trained to undertake ventures and be creative.

The following strategies may be tried in developing cooperative entrepreneurism.

1. Developing the enterprise culture.
2. Evaluating the entrepreneurial competencies.
3. Role of institutions.

1. *Developing Enterprise Culture*

The word "Culture" clearly refers to people's beliefs and attitudes. Enterprise culture can be defined as "a general belief that economic change is both desirable and possible, and that such change can be successfully initiated by individuals as well as by institutions". It is the sum total of individual's attitudes and beliefs and entrepreneurship development programmes aim to change such attitudes and to introduce enterprise culture at the level of the individual participant on the cultural and social aspect. Many of the enterprise development programmes which are provided in countries likes the United Kingdom, have as their objective not only the growth of enterprise and economic activity in general, but also, and often more important, the development of enterprise among a particular ethnic group.

2. *Evaluating Entrepreneurial Competencies*

A competence is an underlying characteristics of a person, which result in effective and/or superior performance in a job. A job competence is an underlying characteristics of a person, in that it may be motive, traits, skills, aspect of ones self-image, a body of knowledge, which one uses. In other words, a competence is a combination of body of knowledge, set of skills and cluster of appropriate motives/traits that an individual possess to perform a given task. Entrepreneurial competencies can be developed by understanding what a particular competence means and, with such an understanding one would be able to recognise the competence when, someone else exhibits the same.

Having understood a competence and having practised the same in a given situation, one needs to introspect to find out how one's "new behaviour" or act of exhibiting a competence has been rewarding. Greater the benefits, more will be one's determination to continue exhibiting the competence in a variety of situations.

The following are the entrepreneurial competencies which may be evaluated among the members of co-operatives who want to become entrepreneurs.

- Initiative
- Sees and acts on opportunities
- Persistence

- Information seeking
- Concern for high quality of works
- Commitment to work contract
- Efficiency-orientation
- Systematic planning
- Problem solving
- Self-confidence
- Assertiveness
- Persuation
- Use of influence strategies
- Monitoring
- Concern for employee welfare.

3. *Role of Institutions*

Both government and non-governmental institutions can extend their guidance and motivation in developing cooperative entrepreneurism through EDP and allied activities. They may include in the following activities.

Training is one way of expanding the entrepreneurial base and motivational training provided during the EDPs to help trainee develop such a personality. Counseling is considered as an important method to help participant to select appropriate business opportunities prepare plans and for effective implementation of the project.

(a) EDP can motivate the trainees and instil in them the confidence to start new co-operative enterprises.

(b) EDPs can provide the necessary opportunities for guidance so that trainees start their enterprises producing marketable goods and services on a commercial levels.

(c) The trained persons are able to solve the problems of production, management, and linkage and stabilise their business.

(*d*) The new entrepreneurial are able to avail the credit facilities from the banks and available support services from the existing development organisations.

(*e*) Finally the new enterprises are able to generate employment opportunities.

The NGO has the opportunity to entrepreneurise the lesser known target group. They may engaged in educating the target group in the area of health, sanitation, education, environment, protection etc.

Moreover the government agencies engaged in this activity may coop and collaborate with NGOs mainly due to sheer magnitude of the operation and their inability to reach the lowest rungs of the society.

Conclusion

At this stage of thinking over the sustainable development of cooperatives it is opt to go for cooperative entrepreneurism. The cooperative principles clubbed with entrepreneurial competencies can pave way for increased economic development of our country. It is sure that if the entrepreneurial culture has been imparted in cooperatives coupled with the efforts of both governmental and non-governmental organisation through EDP will bring great success of the concept, "Cooperative Entrepreneurism" in India.

23

Rural Entrepreneurship: An Emerging Trend

N. Shaik Mohamed

India needs entrepreneurs for two reasons: to capitalise on new opportunities and to create wealth and a new business. The recent McKinsey and Company Report estimates that it needs at least 8,000 new businesses to achieve its target of business a $ 87 billion in IT sector by 2008. Similarly, in the next 10 years, 130 million Indian citizens will be searching for jobs, including 100 million looking for their first jobs; that's seven times Australia's population. Since traditional large employers—including the government and the economy players—may find it difficult to sustain this level of employment in the future, it is entrepreneurs who will create new jobs and opportunities.

Today's knowledge-based economy is a ground to entrepreneurs in India. The success stories of business executed by a talented team have great appeal in India where access to capital is scarce and regulation has often created barriers to success. Estimates indicate that several thousand economy businesses were launched last year in India. When McKinsey Company launched India Venture 2000, a business plan comprised to catalyse entrepreneurship in India, many of the 4,500 teams participated were from small towns such as Meerut, Siliguri, Warangal and Pollachi.

* N. Shaik Mohamed, Reader in Commerce, Jamal Mohamed College, Tiruchirappalli-620 020 Tamil Nadu. e-mail-shaiknaina@yahoo.co.in

India has an extraordinary talent pool to produce entrepreneurs. India must, however commit to creating the right environment to develop successful business builders. The objective of this paper is to highlight the emerging trend in entrepreneurship in rural area.

Right Environment for Success

Entrepreneurs should find it easy to start a business. To do so, most Indians would start slow with capital borrowed from family and friends, the Head playing the role of salesman and strategist. A professional team assembles months or perhaps years after the business was created and few, if any, external partners. A professional management team would drive the business; a multifunctional team would be assembled quickly; and partnerships would be explored early scale up the business.

A first challenge for India is to create a handful of such areas of excellence—the breeding ground where ideas grow into business. Some already exist in a very preliminary way (the business there). For the example, Gurgaon and Hyderabad for remote service, Bangalore for IT services. But these areas of excellence need strengthening before they can claim to be India's own "Valley way of strengthening these areas" is to consider the role of universities and educational institutions—places where excellence typically thrives. Creating such educational institutions by strengthening the Indian Institutes of Technology (IIT's) and some new ones is going to be very important.

Accessibility to Right Skills

A company conducted a survey last year revealed that most of the Indian start-up businesses face two skill gaps: entrepreneurial to manage business risks, build a team, identify and get funding functional (product development know-how, marketing skills). In other countries, entrepreneurs either gain these skills by himself or have access to "support systems" such as universal other institutions that may nurture many regional businesses. In addition, business schools give young graduates the skills and knowledge required for business today. India can move toward ensuring that the curriculum at universally modified to address today's changing business landscape, particularly in emerging markets, and to build 'centres of entrepreneurial excellence' in institutes that will actively assist entrepreneurs.

Indian Business Schools provide a start in developing outstanding entrepreneurial lead. Their program is designed primarily to prepare managers to return to the challenges of rapidly changing business environments. And an environment of intellectual vibrancy, hundreds of students who graduate each year will have studied entrepreneurship, strategic to the impact of technology on commerce. They will have spent on developing their own projects, while utilising state-of-the art communications technology to interact with members of individuals and experts worldwide.

Access to Smart Capital

Indian entrepreneurs have had little access to capital. It is that in the last few years, several Venture Funds have entered into Indian market. And, while the sector is still in its infancy in India (with estimated total disbursements of <$ 0.5 billion last year) is providing capital as well as critical knowledge and access potential partners, suppliers, and clients across the globe. However India has only a few angel investors who support an idea in the stages before Venture Capitals become involved.

Networking and Exchange

Entrepreneurs learn from experience—theirs and that of others. Much of the success of Silicon Valley is attributed to the experience of sharing among members. During the Venture 2000, we were delighted by the eagerness with which established entrepreneurs, who still remembered the challenge faced, offered to support start-ups. Clearly, India would benefit creating a strong network of entrepreneurs and managers that entrepreneurs could draw on for advice and support.

The rapid pace of globalisation and the fast growth of Asian economies present tremendous opportunities and challenges for India.

Through planning and focus, India can aspire to create pool of entrepreneurs who will be the region's and the world leaders of tomorrow.

Conclusion

Thus, rural entrepreneurship in India can be developed by creating right environment, providing accessibility to smart capital, and skills and creating a network of relationship. With the fast growth of global economy, and by developing the above areas, rural entrepreneurship can take off in India in near future.

24

Policy Support and Rural Employment Opportunities

*Mr. S. Sudalai Muthu and Miss. R. Jayapriya**

Introduction

Women constitute almost half of the country's population, which has been deprived of self-respect and subjugated into existence at the whim and mercy of the male. Over the years, women has accepted her role in society as housewife and mothers as well as inferior expendable commodity, whether sold of to strangers or a source of dowry for husband's family. More recently, however protest movements on Global state have brought out the concern that women are an issue.

There is also a general acceptance of the various ways in which women contribute to society and economy. Earlier cultural stereotypes have been scrutinised, a number of new policies, projects and programmes and some form of national machinery for advancement of women have been created. But all this change has not been accompanied by a basic change in state approach to women's issues, which is still limited and biased.

---

* Mr. S. Sudalai Muthu, (HOD of Commerce), and Miss. R. Jayapriya, (Lecturer in Commerce), Vidyasagar College of Arts and Science, Udumalpet-642126.

Self-Help Groups (SHG), (Entrepreneurial Development Programme for Rural Women).

As a consequence number of programmes were launched from time to time for alleviation of rural poverty like extension of credit to priority sectors, development of Khadi and Village Industries, self-employment programmes (IRDP, DWCRA, JRY) etc., but unfortunately, these measures have not really reached the most needy beneficiaries particularly the rural poor women.

The primary and crucial area that can initiate a social and economic change for the elevation of life style of these rural poor women is only through SHG.

Self Help Groups

A small economically homogereous and affinity group of rural/urban, poor, voluntarily formed to save and contribute to a common fund to be lend to its members as per the groups decision and for working target for social and economic uplift of their families and community.

Mission

(+) Let us add our strength.

(-) Subtract our differences.

(×) Multiply our resources.

(/) Divide our responsibilities.

Objectives

The following are the objectives of the SHG Programme.

1. Social Empowerment
2. Economic Empowerment
3. Capacity Building

1. Social Empowerment

(a) Equal status and participation of women to take decisions in household, community and village.

(b) Breaking social, cultural and religious barriers.

(c) Increased status, participation and powers of decision making in democratic institutions.

2. *Economic Empowerment*
   - (a) Greater access to financial resources outside household.
   - (b) Significant increase in the women's own income.
   - (c) Financial self-reliance of women.
3. *Capacity Building*
   - (a) Better awareness on health, education, environment, etc.
   - (b) Improved functional literacy.
   - (c) Better leadership and communication skills.
   - (d) Mutual help.

Organisation Structure

SHG is an unusual long-term partnership between three agencies. The State Government, Non-Government Organisations and NABARD/other banks and financing institutions. The endeavor is to combine the wide reach and resources available to the state, with the grass roots presence, goodwill, commitment and innovative work of the NGO's together with support from NABARD and credit from Banks and other funding sources.

SHG—Salient Features

A major shift of SHG from the erstwhile programme is its emphasis on the social mobilisation of the poor. Social mobilisation enables the poor to build their own organisations viz. SHG's. A SHG may consist of 10-20 persons belonging to families below the poverty line and a person should not be a member of more than opine group. The group members save a regular amount of Rs. 10 to Rs. 100 and more in every month. The group rotates their money to the needy members for various purposes at a specified low rate of interest.

The Government and credit by the bank give assistance under SHG to individual swarozgaris or self-help groups, in the form of subsidy. Credit is the critical component of SHG, subsidy being a minor and enabling element. Accordingly, SHG envisages greater involvement of the banks. Also SHG's can avail the facility of revolving fund of Rs. 10,000 from DRDA and Rs. 15,000 as bank loan, after formation of six months.

Since this project is basically human resource development project training is being given top priority. This scheme provides sufficient training to animators, representatives, etc.

All the activities of SHG's are properly monitored and evaluated by Project Implementation Units, Women Development Cooperation, NGOs and Banks.

The groups, which are engaged in the following activities are eligible to get financial assistance.

1. Candle production
2. Coir making
3. Ration shop
4. Cattle rearing
5. Dairy farm
6. Snacks manufacturing
7. Brass vessels
8. Maligai shop
9. Sericulture
10. Tailoring, etc.

In addition to the above activities SHG's also participate in the social welfare programs like AIDS Awareness Program and Community Health Development Program, etc.

Positive Features

The formation of SHGs has led to the following positive developments, indeed with considerable variation across the groups.

1. SHGs are able to create a variety of credit needs of target group population; something the formal banking system would have not met these credit demands.
2. The quality of credit availed from the SHG is very good.
3. The SHGs have achieved high recovery rates. At the same time, they have reduced dependence on money lenders in the sense that the terms relating to money lending have become somewhat favourable to the poor.
4. They have also brought striking changes in the perception of the poor. It is worth mentioning that the SHGs have brought in new power equations in rural areas, for the target group members are able to meet credit requirements on their own without depending heavily on the rural elite.

Conclusion

Thus the formation of SHGs has led to a number of positive features. The most important achieved aspect is that the earlier belief that the poor are unbankable and less credit worthy has been proven wrong. Most of the earlier studies reveal that the poor can excel in gaining access to management and is assuming control over their own financial resources and too can help themselves in their social, economic and political development given opportunities and professional encouragement.

25

Micro Finance and Rural Development

Tanya Johnson

India is a developing country. She lives in villages as the major portion of Indian population i.e. 74.28% is living in 5,76,126 villages. The standard of living of all these villages continue to be poor from the time prior to independence till today. So the development of all these villages assumes great significance. Even after half a century of development efforts initiated by the state, the problems of poverty, hunger, malnutrition and unemployment, gender inequality and illiteracy plague the Indian society. Therefore in order to change the face of the socio-economic environment, Micro Enterprises played an important role in the self employment and entrepreneurship and in raising the level of income and standard of living among the people especially the rural poor and the weaker sections. The lack of credit support had led the entrepreneurs to depend on money lenders who charge high rates of interest. In view of their importance, banks and financial institutions have evolved the Micro Credit and Micro Finance Schemes.

Definition

The most acceptable definition of Micro Finance is "the provision of thrift credit and other financial services and products of very small amount to the poor in rural, semi-urban and urban areas to enable them to raise their income levels and improve their standard of living."

Features

Micro Finance is distinctly different from other poverty alleviation schemes and should not be misunderstood as just small loans. Micro Finance has some important features:

1. Loans made are very small and on an average less than $ 100 according to world standards and Rs. 100 by Indian standards.
2. Micro Finance targets rural and urban households and lays emphasis on women borrowers, provision of finance for creation of assets and their bringing greater quality of services. Beneficiaries are identified by Micro Finance providers or NGOs.
3. Formation of homogeneous groups by individuals themselves, followed by the mobilisation of petty savings and recycling this by lending to group members.
4. Repayment period is generally very short and is based on the loan graduation process.
5. Provision of credit to the poor through financial institutions at subsidised rates.
6. RBI has not imposed any ceiling on the loan amount.
7. The Operational Strategy involves simple procedures for reviewing and approving loan application, delivery of credit and related services at commercial rates of interest in a convenient and user friendly way, clear recovery procedures and strategies, incentives to access larger loans immediately following repayment of first loan.
8. Micro Finance focuses on the process retaining all earlier characteristics. The new paradigm emphasises financial intermediation with self sustainability of institutions and quantitative/qualitative out reach to the poor.

Emergence of Micro Finance

India has the problem of mass poverty as major portion of Indian society is lacking the basic necessities of life and lives below the poverty line. The need of the hour was sought to be rural development. To bridge the wide gap between the demand and supply of funds in the lower rungs of the rural economy, the formal sector took the initiative to develop a supplementary credit delivery mechanism by encouraging institutional arrangements outside the financial system. With the launch of NABARD's pilot scheme—Micro Finance-the development buzzword of the 1990's gained visibility in the Indian development landscape to cure the illness of rural poverty.

Micro Finance emerged as an effective strategy for institutional financing agencies, as:

- group lending minimises the transaction cost.
- it can make small loans through the group.
- chances of misutilisation are rare.
- there is assured repayment because of peer monitoring by the group and the whole group is liable for the amount borrowed from the bank.
- group concept has enabled them to create the habit of thrift and thereby minimise extravagance.

Role of Intermediaries

RBI has encouraged the banks to extend credit to individual borrowers directly or through intermediaries. Banks can start with any Micro Credit Organisation in a selected small area and concentrate fully on the poor in that area and then replicate the arrangement in other selected areas.

NABARD introduced a scheme in 1992 where in the Self Help Groups (SHGs) were linked with the banks in order to strengthen and improve the financial position of SHGs. NABARD started providing support services in the area of capacity building, training and promotion of SHGs to a limited extent as financial intermediaries also.

Through the establishment of the SHGs, the NGOs play a catalytic role in building social capital that can generate a sound base for their members to develop their credibility as borrowers and encourage financial institutions (NABARD/

SIDBI/IDBI) to develop confidence in lending to the groups. NGOs has trained and developed the SHGs to a level where it can do business on equal terms with the bank. Social and communication barriers often make it necessary for the NGOs to foster the relationship between the SHG and the bank for some time.

Besides the SHG-Bank linkage programme, several other Micro Finance Institutions (MFIs) function with the assistance from external donors or on the strength of individual savings. Loans are also provided to NGOs for lending to SHG members. The NGO sector is pursuing their financial intermediation as one of the effective tools in meeting their social agenda. Thus the Government both at the Centre and at the State have equally important role to play in the growth of this NGO sector as future Micro Financing Institutions.

Grameen Bank Model

An excellent model of micro finance was the Grameen Bank (GB) of Bangladesh in the context of rural development and poverty alleviation. This model had made waves across the globe and some developing countries have replicated this model to tackle the problems of poverty in their countries. The GB received worldwide attention mainly due to the group lending and repayment incentives. Successful group members have an incentive to repay the loans of group members whose project have yielded insufficient return to make repayment worthwhile.

The banks average loan limit is Rs. 100 per day and the members have to attend weekly meetings and repay the instalments on time, failure of which may lead to a fine or even expelling a member for lack of observance of rules. They never go to the courts or police, rather the bank's business is based on free communication, good relations and mutual trust. This GB model has a fair chance of reducing poverty in the rural areas of any country.

Though the real scenario of poverty has not changed much, it offers a solution to tackle the twin problems of poverty and unemployment. It can train the poor on income generating activities as a easier way rather than depending upon the Government.

Current Scenario

In 1999 there were about 33000 SHGs with 5.6 lacs micro entrepreneurs with an amount of Rs. 57 crores of outstanding loan under the schemes. It has been estimated that by the year 2003 nearly 200,000 SHGs would be linked with the banks and many NGOs will transform themselves into Micro Financing Institutions (MFIs).

In order to examine and address various critical issues for a healthy and orderly growth of the Micro Finance Sector in the country, a Task Force was set up by NABARD with members drawn from various MFIs, banks, NGOs, RBI and Government. The Task Force has advocated a National Policy for Micro Finance for building the capacities of the poor in the management of sustainable self-employment activities besides providing them other financial services like savings, consumption credit, housing and insurance.

Conclusion

It can be thus observed that Micro Finance is a novel way to extend credit to the rural poor and a strategic tool for poverty alleviation and rural development. If the Grameen Bank model is repeated in Indian villages, it will ensure multiple benefits for the rural economy. One of the major contributions of Micro Finance is towards women's empowerment. Further focus on rural women will have to be continued in all Micro Financing Programme activities. Another important feature that is to be noted is that, the basic principles of prudent banking have been adhered to and the traditional forms of loan evaluation while delivering finance have been totally ignored.

Bibliography

1. Third Concept, January 2003.
2. Economic and Political Weekly, Vol. xxxviii No. 5, February 2003.
3. Kurukshetra, Vol. 50 No. 4, February 2002.
4. Southern Economist, Vol. 41, No. 10, September 2002
5. Kisan World, Vol 29 No. 6, June 2002.

26

Government Assistance for the Entrepreneurship Development in the Rural Area

*Dr. M. Manoharan**

*Dr. A. Ramachandren***

Introduction

The basic objective of the Industrial Policy framed by the Tamil Nadu Government is to achieve massive increase in employment by promoting small and Rural Industries. The government is of the firm belief that given the magnitude of unemployment and the number of persons living below the poverty line, the touch stone of all industrial schemes and investments ought to be their employment potential, especially in the short term.

For this purpose a thrust has been given to establish, promote and develop the rural industries which are also called the cottage industries and village industries or small industries including tiny and house hold sector, particularly in backward areas where it is essentially needed.

The policies and programme of government for the development of rural industrialisation based on the utilisation of local resources and raw materials and locally availed

* Dr. M. Manoharan, Reader in Commerce, C.P.A College, Bodinayakanur.

** Dr. A. Ramachandren, Selection Grade Lecturer in Economics, C.P.A College, Bodinayakanur.

manpower and skill are translated in to action through the various agencies under the Industries Department which are primarily concerned with the promotion of small and Rural Industries. Provisions have been made to provide infrastructure facilities. Support assistance is provided and growth centers have been promoted. Institutions like Tamil Nadu Industrial Investment Corporation (TIIC) along with Small Industries Service Institute of India (SISI) and nationalised banks assume the responsibility for providing necessary inputs to this sector. This will go a long way in reducing unemployment.

The various agencies and their schemes on subsidies are discussed below.

1. *District Industries Centres*

The District Industries Centre is the Institution at the District level which provides all the services and support facilities to the entrepreneur for setting up Small and Village Industries.

This included identification of suitable schemes, preparation of feasibility reports, arrangements for credit facilities, machinery and equipments, provision of raw materials and extension services.

Subsidies granted by DIC

Granting 15 per cent state capital subsidies for industries set up in backward areas and 20 per cent for most backward areas.

Granting 20 per cent special capital subsidy for the specified industries irrespective of areas.

Granting 5 per cent additional capital subsidy for the industry, which employs more than 30 per cent of women employees.

Granting 15 per cent subsidy for the purchase of new generators.

Granting subsidy on low-tension power tariff @ 40 per cent, 30 per cent and 20 per cent for the first three years respectively.

Granting export compensatory subsidy for Leather and Electronic Industries.

2. *New Anna Marumalarchi Thittam*

The Government of Tamil Nadu is keen on promoting industrial investment in rural areas under small scale sector particularly on agro based industries in order to have employment generation in rural areas.

Having understood the fact that the engine of industrial growth lies in agro business sector, the Government have announced a scheme called "New Anna Marumalarchi Thittam" wherein the Government direct that the scheme shall be implemented in 385 blocks of the state. Small scale industrial units not exceeding three agro-based economic activity with a minimum capital investment of Rs. 1 Crore and more with the capacity to generate employment would be encouraged in each of the 385 blocks in the State under the scheme.

3. *Technology Upgradation Fund*

The Government appealed SSI sector to come out with quality products with international standards for which the Government has announced a package on 30th August 2000 viz. Technology Upgradation Fund which will attract 12% backend subsidy for the loans obtained for the purposes irrespective of area of location of the units 12% backend subsidy would be admissible on the loan advanced by the Scheduled Banks/specified State Finance Corporations to the selected category of small scale industries sectors, viz

1. Leather and leather products including footwear and garments.
2. Food processing,
3. Information Technology (Hard ware),
4. Drugs and Pharmaceuticals,
5. Auto spareparts and components,
6. Electronic Industry particularly relating to designs measurings,

7. Glass and ceramic items including tiles,
8. Dyes and intermediates,
9. Toys
10. Tyres
11. Hand tools
12. Bicycle parts and
13. Found areas—ferrous and cost iron.

Government has ear-marked Rs. 600 crores towards this cause and the scheme has come into operation from 1-10-2000 and will remain till 30-9-2005 i.e., for 5 years Period (or) till the sanction of capital subsidy by modal agency i.e., SIDBI Small Industries Development Bank of India, reaches 600 crores which is earlier.

According to the procedure of the scheme, the lending institutions viz. the Scheduled Bank and specified State Finance Corporations would be required to lodge claims of capital subsidy from SIDBI on a quarterly basis. SIDBI will settle the claim expeditiously.

The scheme has been so devised that the landing institution/SIDBI would ensure preference to tiny sector for loans for technology upgradation. The entrepreneurs availing credit linked capital subsidy for technology upgradation shall not availed any other benefit including interest subsidy under any other scheme of Central Government.

4. *Agricultural and Processed Foods Export Development Authority*

The Agricultural and Processed Food Products Exports Development Authority (APEDA) came into existence in 1986 to further develop our agricultural commodities and processed foods and to promote their exports. Its goals is to maximize foreign exchange earnings through increased agro exports, to provide better income to the farmers through higher unit value realisation and to create employment opportunities in rural areas by encouraging value added exports of farm produce.

Assistance Schemes of Apeda-APEDA offers financial assistance under various schemes. They are

Components	Scale
(a) They are assistance for purchase of specialised transport units for meat, horticulture and floriculture sector.	25% of the cost subject to a ceiling of Rs. 2.50 lakhs per beneficiary.
(b) Assistance to exporters/producers/growers/cooperative organisation and federations.	
(i) Mechanisation of harvest operation of the produce	50% of the cost subject to a ceiling of Rs. 5 lakhs per beneficiary.
(ii) Purchases of intermediate packaging material for domestic transporation of produce.	50% of the cost of equipment subject to a ceiling of Rs. 5.00 lakhs per beneficiary.
(iii) Setting up of sheds for intermediate storage and grading/storage/cleaning operation of	50% of the cost of equipment subject to a ceiling of Rs. 500 lakhs per produce beneficiary.
(iv) (a) Setting up of mechanised handing facilities including sorting, grading, washing, waxing, packaging and palletisation.	50% of the cost of equipment subject to a ceiling of Rs. 10.00 lakhs per beneficiary.
(b) Setting up of pre cooling facilities with proper air handling system.	50% of the cost of equipment subject to a ceiling of Rs. 10.00 lakhs per beneficiary.
(c) Providing facilities for preshipment treatment such as fumigation, X-Ray Screening, hot water dip treatment.	25% of the cost of equipment subject to a ceiling of Rs. 10.00 lakhs per beneficiary.
(d) Setting up of vapour heat treatment, electronic beam processing irradiation facilities.	50% of the cost subject to a ceiling of Rs. 50 lakhs per beneficiary.
(e) Assistance for setting up of environment control system (e.g.) pollution control, effluent treatment, etc.	50% of the cost subject to a ceiling of Rs. 50 lakhs per beneficiary.
(f) Setting up of specialised storage facilities such as high humidity cold storage, deep freezers, controlled atmosphere (CA) or modified atmosphere (MA) storage.	50% of the cost subject to a ceiling of Rs. 50.00 lakhs per beneficiary.

27

Role of District Industries Centre in Promoting Rural Entrepreneurism

*R. Jeyabalan**

Introduction

In order to create a congenial climate for the smooth development of Small Scale Industries (SSI), various policy frame works have been formulated by the Department of Small Scale Industries and Agro and Rural Industries (Ministry of Industries, Government of India). The measures and programmes envisaged by the apex body include the setting up of a network of institutions to render assistance and to provide a comprehensive range of services and facilities for SSI units. The range of services covers consultancy in techno-economic and managerial aspects, training and testing facilities and marketing assistance through the agencies created for such specified function. These activities are supported by a host of other government departments both at the centre and at the state level, promotional agencies, autonomous institution, non-government organisations and the like which provide support to small-scale industrial units in different ways.

District Industries Centre (DIC)

Though a number of measures have been taken for the development of small and village industries by various

* R. Jeyabalan, S.G. Lecturer in Commerce, C.P.A. College, Bodinayakanur.

governments, the actual achievements in the field have been far below the expectation. Also the focus of attention for industrial development was mainly on large cities and state capitals to the neglect of district areas. In addition, multiplicity of institutions involved in small industries development and complicated systems and procedures made the job of promoting the industrial units an uphill task for small entrepreneurs. Hence, it was felt necessary to establish a development agency, which could provide all services and facilities to village and small industries under one roof. Accordingly the DICs were established in May 1978 in order to cater to the needs of small units.

Each district has a DIC at its headquarters. The main aim of DIC is to act as the chief co-ordinator of multifunctional agency in respect of various government departments and other agencies. The prospective small entrepreneurs would get all assistance from DIC for setting up and running in industry in rural areas. The metropolitan cities of Delhi, Mumbai, Kolkata and Chennai have been kept outside the purview of DIC.

Organisational Structure of DIC

The organisational structure of a DIC consists of one general manager, four functional managers and three project managers to provide technical services in the area relevant to provide technical services in the area relevant to the needs of the districts concerned. The management of DIC is done by the state government.

Functions of DIC

Identification of Entrepreneurs: DIC develops new entrepreneurs by conducting entrepreneurs motivation programmes throughout the district especially in panchayat union headquarters and small towns.

Selection of Projects: It offers technical advice to new entrepreneurs for the selection of projects suitable to them.

Provisional Registration Under SSI: After the selection of projects, entrepreneurs are issued with provisional

SSI Registration, which is essential for obtaining assistance from the financial institutions.

Purchase of Fixed Assets: DIC sponsors the loan application to TIIC, SIDCO and/or banks for the purchase of land and buildings and sanctions margin money under Rural Industries Project Loan Scheme payable to other financial agencies for the purchase of plant and machinery.

Clearance from Various Departments: It takes the initiative to get clearance from various departments and takes follow up measures to get speedy power connection.

Assistance to Raw Material Supplies: It makes recommendations to the concerned raw material suppliers and issues the required certificates for the import of raw material and machinery wherever necessary.

Assistance to Village Artisans and Handicrafts: DIC arranges for the financial assistance with lead bank of the respective areas. Interest-free sales tax loan: SSI units setup in rural areas can get IFST loan up to a maximum limit of eight per cent of the total fixed assets form SIDCO. But the sanction order from the same is being issued by DIC. The DIC also recommends SSI units to NSIC for registration for Government purchase programme.

Subsidy Schemes: DIC assists SSI units and rural artisans to get subsidy for engineers, subsidy under IRDP and the like from various institutions.

Training Programmes: DIC gives training to rural entrepreneurs and also assists other units giving training to small entrepreneurs.

Self Employment for Unemployed Educated Youth: This scheme was introduced in 1983-84 for youth between 18 years and 25 years with SSLC. Technocrats and women are given preference.

Conclusion

District Industries Centres are supposed to provide pre-investment and post-investment assistance to entrepreneurs under one roof. The services preformed by them to their clients are crucial. Success of many new small entrepreneurs depends up on how effectively they are guided, how efficiently they are followed up and how prudentially they are encouraged by the authorities like DIC. In fact, DICs, are playing a leading role in industrial development in rural India.